The Writer's Journey

The Writer's Journey

In the Footsteps of the Literary Greats

Travis Elborough

WHITE LION PUBLISHING

Contents

Introduction

The French literary theorist Roland Barthes once wrote an essay entitled 'The Writer on Holiday' in which he mused on the seeming impossibility of authors to ever completely down tools, even while relaxing on a sandy beach or journeying down the Congo. 'By having holidays', he wrote, the writer 'displays the sign of his being human; but the god remains, one is a writer as Louis XIV was a king, even on the commode.' If life for all of us is a journey of sorts, journeys for writers are, by this reckoning, simply further sources of fresh material. Yet a change of scene can really work wonders on the creative imagination. As this book hopefully illustrates, some truly remarkable works of literature have been produced either in response to a place visited or as a direct result of a writer's time away from their typical surroundings or by a writer's embrace of a new life in a new country.

Authors and poets often travel quite expressly with the purpose of producing a piece or book. You will find plenty of examples here of writers' journeys that fall into that category. Though as you will also see, there were frequently unintended consequences from such odysseys on the writers' later output. These journeys, in some instances, would alter the entire course of the writers' careers. In other instances, the trip would be the very thing that turned them into a writer; the immersion in a different landscape, encounters with other peoples and unfamiliar transport, customs, food, drink, weather, insects, cafés, bars and hotels all providing the raw material and a store of memories that could subsequently – and profitably – be mined in print. Going away someplace else can also give authors the time, distance and space they need to write, with a few friendly locals and similarly minded, artistically inclined fellow expats thrown in for good measure.

The world is a good deal less difficult to navigate today than it was in centuries past and the sights, sounds and flavours of other countries are easy to obtain in our digitally connected, globalized present. Until comparatively recently, travel could be extremely arduous and expensive and came with substantial risks. Locals and hoteliers were not always friendly. Before steam- and petrol-powered propulsion, wooden sailing ships were at the mercy of the weather and in constant danger of being wrecked (a couple of the writers you'll meet here had brushes with the possibility of a watery death). Disease, too, posed a threat to the life of the wandering scribe, as even Grand Tours of antique lands came with the risk of possibly succumbing to cholera or catching malaria. Sadly dysentery proved fatal to one of the most peripatetic of writers in this book.

Some of the writers who appear in the pages to follow were quite literally journeying into the unknown or, at least, straying into territories whose maps were sketchy and that few others concerned themselves with. At the other end of the scale, as commercially successful professionals with bestsellers under their belts, there are one or two writers here who ventured forth in some style, journeying first class, dining at captains' tables and in the best restaurants and staying in only the finest hotels to be found on their respective itineraries. It's fair to say that several of the authors here have helped put certain destinations on the tourist map simply by writing about them and encouraging others to follow in their footsteps – or those of their characters. Literary pilgrims, after all, have long sought out the real locations utilized in fiction by their favourite authors, as well as the haunts once favoured by their bookish idols when they toiled on future masterpieces far from home.

Ultimately, then, this is an atlas dedicated to writers who went the distance; and the places, near and far, that stirred their creativity in one way or another. Their ambits are mapped with lines on paper (both mine and those of the cartographer). Our coordinates are set by their directions of travel. But while ports of call can easily be plotted they only tell part of the story; the writers' journeys featured here had enormous repercussions for their personal lives and the broader literary landscape. In sharing these travellers' tales, we hope you find the journeys as pleasurable as the end destination.

Andersen's Journey to Italy

DENMARK

GERMANY

FRANCE

SWITZERLAND

ITALY

1 Copenhagen
2 Paris
3 Le Locle
4 Rome
5 Naples
6 Capri

N

0   100   200 km

0   50   100 mi

Hans Christian Andersen Becomes a Novelist in Italy

The ungainly, illegitimate offspring of a short-lived marriage between a bookish shoemaker and a near-illiterate washerwoman, Hans Christian Andersen (1805–1875) was to identify with outsiders all his life. Mocked for his height and girlish voice and demeanour, he was sent out to earn money as a child, toiling in a cloth mill and a tobacco factory to help support his widowed mother. Her subsequent remarriage and his admittance to a charity school in Odense, the Danish city of his birth, saved him from a career of demeaning manual labour. Not content to languish in a provincial backwater, Andersen travelled to Copenhagen in 1828 and succeeded in finding patrons for his studies at the city's university. A year later, while still a student, Andersen enjoyed his first flush of literary success, publishing a fantastic tale in the vein of the German Romantic writer E.T.A. Hoffmann, after which he began to write for the theatre.

In 1833, and following a fruitful trip to Germany two years earlier, Andersen was able to embark on a lengthy sojourn abroad thanks to the financial backing of wealthy admirers. The bulk of this excursion was to be spent in Italy, which he had yearned to visit after reading Johann Wolfgang von Goethe's *Italian Journey* and Madame de Staël's *Corinne, or Italy*, a popular novel of the period.

Andersen left Copenhagen on 22 April 1833 and was not to return until 3 August 1834. Paris was his first destination; he spent three months in the French capital and met Victor Hugo for the first time. On 15 August 1833, he departed for Switzerland, staying in Le Locle, just over the mountain border from France, for the next three weeks. Such alpine scenery would later come to inform one of his best-known fairy tales, *The Ice Maiden*. Andersen finally entered Italy on 19 September, and reached Rome on 18 October, where he was to remain until 12 February 1834.

Rome was, arguably, to alter the course of his career. For it was there, stimulated by the sights and sounds of a city of rococo Catholic churches and ancient temples, that he began to write *The Improvisatore*. This debut novel, a semi-autobiographical rags-to-artistic-and-emotional-riches *Bildungsroman*, was to be the basis of Andersen's early fame. One of the most significant details of the book was that Andersen was to make its hero, Antonio, an Italian singer raised in poverty in Rome, his birthplace the corner of piazza Barberini and via Felice, within sight of Gian Lorenzo Bernini's Triton Fountain.

Other elements of the city's topography, from the Spanish Steps to the Colosseum, were to be tapped for backdrops in the novel. For instance, young

Antonio has his first encounter with a guitar-toting *improvisatore* (a street performer) near the Trevi Fountain. The nine-year-old Antonio's own vocal gifts, meanwhile, are revealed in a scene that unfolds in the icon-stuffed church of Santa Maria in Ara Coeli on the summit of the Campidoglio, a site that Andersen himself visited with Henrik Hertz, another visiting Danish writer, on 27 December 1833.

In the new year, Andersen, accompanied by Hertz, headed south, reaching Naples on 16 February 1834. The heat and louche atmosphere of this port, whose thoroughfares thronged with sailors, singers, card sharks, pimps and prostitutes, seem almost instantaneously to have aroused Hertz's libido. After three days in the city, Andersen wrote in his diary about having been approached by pimps offering their *bella donnas* and reported, 'I've noticed that the climate is affecting my blood – I felt a raging passion but resisted.' Hertz, it is made plain, was incapable of such denial in the face of Neapolitan temptation.

Another thing that excited both men was Mount Vesuvius, east of Naples, which erupted on one of their first evenings in the city. Andersen recorded hearing 'a sudden ... strange sound in the air, like when several doors are slammed all at once, but with a supernatural power'. He rushed to a nearby square to get a better view, and later scaled the mountain to look into its burning crater. The nearby ruins of Herculaneum and Pompeii also left a deep impression on the writer. They, like Naples and Vesuvius, were to appear in *The Improvisatore*, Antonio's interests and itineraries, predictably perhaps, closely mapping Andersen's own.

Again in the novel, Antonio stuns audiences with a performance in Naples' Teatro di San Carlo, the opera house where Andersen was to watch a spellbinding turn by the legendary contralto-soprano Maria Malibran in the title role in Vincenzo Bellini's *Norma* on 23 February. Malibran would supply the writer with the inspiration for the character of Antonio's first love, Annunziata.

One further place was to prove pivotal to the book, with Andersen using Antonio's return visit to the island of Capri's Grotta Azzurra, or Blue Grotto, to close the novel. The grotto, which lies inside a rocky cavern that can only be reached through a small opening in the cliff, and once served as a private bathing pool for Emperor Tiberius, had only recently been rediscovered by the outside world when Andersen himself visited in March 1834. For Danes and Scandinavians, the grotto became an almost sacred place of literary pilgrimage, with hundreds flocking to see for themselves the fairy world Andersen had described 'where all gleamed like the ether' and water was 'like a blue burning fire'.

Andersen wended his way back to Rome for Easter Week, and after that passed through Florence and Venice to Vienna and Munich. After Italy, the writer confessed he had neither 'the mind nor heart for Germany', while even the thought of Denmark left him feeling fear and distress. But return he did, to finish *The Improvisatore* and prepare his first two booklets of fairy tales for publication. All three were to appear within months of one another in 1835. While *The Improvisatore* would bring the Dane fame, it was the fairy stories, as he'd been presciently assured by one astute critic, that would make him immortal.

▶ TOP Rome.

▶ BOTTOM *The Blue Grotto on the Island of Capri*, watercolour painting by Jakob Alt, c.1835.

Maya Angelou Loses Her Heart to Ghana

Maya Angelou (1928–2014) had an artistic output that ranged from poetry and folksy stories to powerful autobiography and memoir. She also had a singing and acting career, which included touring in a production of *Porgy and Bess* and becoming Hollywood's first Black female director, and was a prominent activist in the civil rights movement of the late 1950s and 1960s. Her work as a coordinator in Dr Martin Luther King, Jr's Southern Christian Leadership Conference organization was eventually to lead her to leave the United States for Africa.

Angelou settled for nearly two years in Cairo with her son, Guy, and husband Vusumzi Make, a South African anti-apartheid campaigner who was serving as the representative of the Pan Africanist Congress (PAC) in Egypt. When their brief marriage ended in 1962, Angelou accepted the offer of a post in the Ministry of Information in Liberia. Before that, however, she planned to travel to Ghana with her son, who was to enrol at the University of Accra. Within days of their arrival in Accra, though, Guy was injured in a car accident, the fault of a drunken driver, and Angelou was forced to stay on to look after him. As Angelou was later to write in *All God's Children Need Traveling Shoes*, the fifth volume of her autobiography and the book that covers her time in Ghana, she'd ended up in staying in the country 'by accident, literally'.

This west African nation on the coast of the Gulf of Guinea had only obtained its independence from Britain in 1957. Its first president was the charismatic Marxist Kwame Nkrumah, who believed his country would usher in the end of colonial rule across Africa. The whole continent, or so he hoped, would unite under socialism once freed from imperial oppressors. Educated at Lincoln University in Pennsylvania, USA, Nkrumah had issued an extended welcome to any African-Americans wishing to emigrate to Ghana and harboured political refugees fleeing white rule in south and eastern Africa. Despite the job waiting for her in Liberia, Angelou decided to stick around. Finally, she and her son were in a place where, as she put it, 'for the first time in our lives the color of our skin was accepted as correct and normal.'

Angelou obtained an office admin position at the Institute of African Studies at the university, and started immersing herself in Accra's cultural life, getting to know the author, playwright and actor Julian Mayfield (a Black American émigré who'd left the United States to escape the attentions of the CIA and the FBI) and Efua Sutherland, a poet, playwright, teacher and head of The National Theatre of Ghana. Angelou was soon pitching in at the theatre, taking bookings and selling tickets at the box office, and was later to appear on its stage in the lead role of Bertolt Brecht's *Mother Courage and Her Children*.

Alongside her day job, Angelou began writing articles for the *Ghanaian Times*, bonding with the paper's editor over a shared preference for the local Club beer over the rival Ghanaian brand of Star.

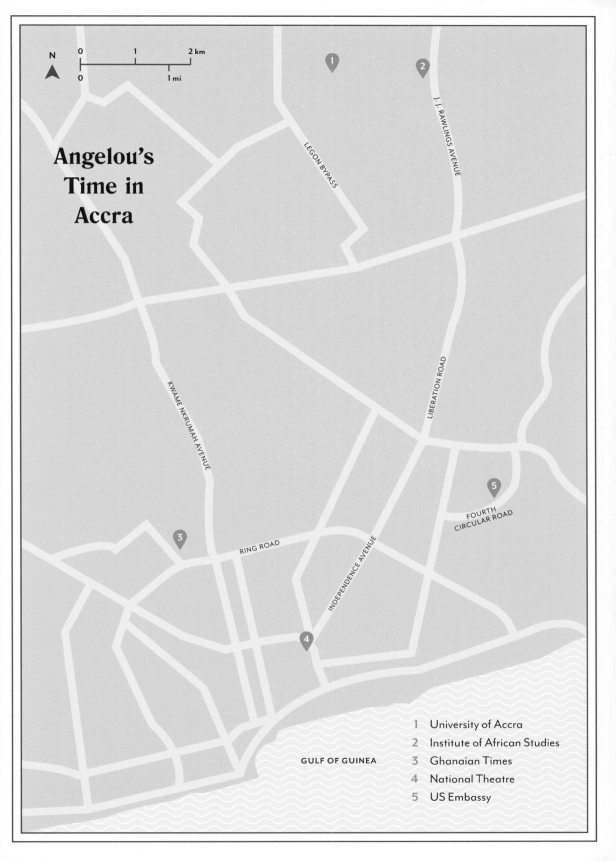

When it was announced that Dr Martin Luther King, Jr planned to lead a march on Washington, DC for jobs and freedom on 28 August 1963 – an historic event in the struggle for civil rights that would see some 250,000 people gathering in front of the Lincoln Memorial and that concluded with King delivering his immortal 'I Have a Dream' speech – Angelou was among the organizers of a sister march in Accra. The Ghanaian version was to parade past the American embassy to show solidarity with the cause, though in order to run in sync with King's march it had to begin at midnight due to the time difference.

While Angelou was in Ghana, two other major figures in the struggle for civil rights in the United States were to pitch up in Accra: the boxer Muhammad Ali and Angelou's friend Malcolm X, the fiery orator of Black liberation. Malcolm X had been on something of journey himself. Having undertaken a pilgrimage to Mecca, he had broken with his one-time mentor Elijah Muhammad of the Nation of Islam. If Malcolm was treated to an audience with Nkrumah, he was cold-shouldered by Ali when their paths crossed in Ghana for forsaking Elijah.

If happy in Ghana, Angelou was to observe the tensions between the African-American incomers and the indigenous population, and equally some of the disparities in the lifestyles enjoyed by Nkrumah's officials and those of the ordinary citizens. Language was one significant separating factor between the émigrés and the Ghanaians and Angelou took it upon herself to learn Fante.

After two years in Ghana, Angelou felt the pull of home. Reading of events in the United States in the letters she received from Malcolm X, who had now formed his Organization of Afro-American Unity, she sensed that her country could be on the cusp of great change and decided to return home to play her part in the struggle. Encouraged by James Baldwin, her writing, both verse and prose, would become an

instrument with which she gave expression to that cause and to the experiences of Black people, especially in the wake of the assassinations of both Malcolm X and Dr King. Ghana, though, had been a vital staging post on her personal and creative journey. As she was to maintain: 'If the heart of Africa still remained elusive, my search for it had brought me closer to understanding myself and other human beings.'

◀ Accra, Ghana.

▼ Kwame Nkrumah's Mausoleum, Kwame Nkrumah Memorial Park, Accra.

1 Li Kwo Yi
2 Lake Tai
3 Shanghai
4 Hankou
5 Jujiang (Kiukiang)
6 Nanchang
7 Huangshan City (Tunki)
8 Jinhua (Kin-hwa)
9 Wenzhou
10 Guangzhou (Canton)
11 Hong Kong

N
0   100   200 km
0   50   100 mi

CHINA

**Auden and
Isherwood's Tour
of China**

W.H. Auden and Christopher Isherwood Go to War

Following the positive reception to *Letters from Iceland*, a travel book in verse and prose that W.H. Auden (1907–1973) had written with Louis MacNeice, based on the two poets' trip to Iceland in 1936, Auden was invited by his American publisher to supply a follow-up volume about the East, eventually to be titled *Journey to a War*. This time he'd be collaborating with Christopher Isherwood (1904–1986), his old friend and occasional lover, the pair having just produced a play together, *The Ascent of F6*, which had a pseudo-Asian setting.

Auden, like his near contemporary George Orwell, had been moved by the political situation in Spain to go to Barcelona in January 1937, with the aim of volunteering as an ambulance driver to support the republican cause. But thwarted in his various attempts to help out, and horrified by infighting of the various leftist factions and the wanton destruction of the city's churches, he returned to Britain barely two months later, completely disheartened by what he'd seen. That summer, just as Auden and Isherwood were mulling over plans for their travel book, news reached them that the Japanese army, which had been encroaching on Chinese territory since seizing Manchuria in 1931, had invaded southward from Beijing (then Peking) and was attacking Shanghai. China, as Isherwood would later remember, 'had now become one of the world's decisive battlegrounds' and they decided that they should go there and write about it. 'And

unlike Spain', as they somewhat cynically also surmised, 'it wasn't already crowded with star literary observers'. Auden, in the recollection Isherwood set down decades later in his memoir *Christopher and His Kind*, allegedly remarked that, 'We'll have a war all of our very own.' This didn't prove to be strictly true. The travel writer Peter Fleming and the famous war photographer Robert Capa were among the Western luminaries who Auden and Isherwood would run into on their travels.

For Auden, as for Isherwood, this was to be their first journey 'to any place east of Suez'. Neither spoke Chinese, nor, as they readily admitted, did either of them possess any 'special knowledge of Far Eastern Affairs'. But interest in this foray into the hazardous field of war reporting by two literary men ensured that a phalanx of reporters and press photographers was waiting for them at Victoria Station in London when they boarded their boat train to Dover on 19 January 1938.

After spending an evening in Paris, the writers journeyed south to Marseilles and sailed two days later on the *Aramis*. When the passenger ship docked in Port Said in Egypt, they got off and a spent the day exploring Cairo before rejoining their vessel at Port Tewfik after it had cleared the Suez Canal. From here the *Aramis* pursued a steady course southward, via Djibouti, Colombo in Sri Lanka, Singapore and Ho Chi Minh City (then Saigon) in Vietnam, until it reached Hong Kong on 16 February. The

◀ Christopher Isherwood and
W.H. Auden on board the
Dover-bound boat train,
London, 19 January 1938.

▶ Nanchang, China.

In Li Kwo Yi they faced opposition from
General Chang Tschen to their attempts to get to
the frontline. Similarly, at Huangshan City (then
Tunki) their path to the action near Lake Tai was
obstructed by an officious newspaperman, Mr Kao,
and permission to head further north to observe the
Eighth Route Army in action was refused, forcing
them to retreat down the Chang Jiang (Yangtze
River) to Hankou (one of three cities that later
merged to form the city of Wuhan).

Auden and Isherwood were assisted for most
of their travels by their 'boy', Chiang, an amiable
middle-aged Chinese guide put at their disposal
by the consul in Hankou, their first port of call
after Guangzhou and reached by one of the many
painfully slow trains. At Hankou, Isherwood and
Auden watched a Japanese air raid while lying flat
on their backs on the lawn of the British Consulate
building. Their relaxed pose in the face of possible
annihilation was adopted, at Auden's suggestion,
to avoid them getting stiff necks.

Encountering 'real' war correspondents,
Isherwood felt compelled to confess that they were
'mere trippers' and dilettante amateurs. But the pair
did experience moments of genuine danger, such as
when they were left perilously exposed on a visit to
the front at Han Chiang, the Japanese choosing to
return fire while they were crossing an open field.

Some respite was supplied, though, when they
journeyed by river steamer to Jiujiang (then Kiukiang)
and upon arrival were promptly whisked off by
car to the Journey's End Hotel in the Guling (then
Kuling) Hills by its characterful English proprietor,
Mr Charleston. From Jiujiang they ventured to

writers received a red-carpet welcome to the British
colony from government officials, but deemed the
city 'hideous' and a 'Victorian colonial fortress'
comprised of clashing architectural styles. Neither
were its British inhabitants much more appealing.

On 28 February, Auden and Isherwood left
Hong Kong on a riverboat for Guangzhou (then
Canton). Their choice of transport was dictated
by the fact that the Japanese were now bombing
the Kowloon–Canton railway daily. This riverboat
journey was the start of three and a half months of
protracted 'wanderings around China', encountering
American missionaries, White Russian exiles and
countless other non-native eccentrics alongside the
Chinese themselves. The writers' course was ever
shifting, as they faced delays and diversions caused
by the manoeuvres of the Japanese in concert with
the obstructive tactics of Chinese government
and military functionaries keen to keep Western
journalists at arm's length.

Shexian, Huangshan City
(then Tunki), China.

Nanchang, then took a train to Jinhua (then Kin-hwa) and went by bus to Wenzhou, where another river steamer awaited to carry them to Shanghai, which they arrived at on 25 May.

In Shanghai they accepted an invitation to stay in the International Settlement at the home of the pipe-smoking British ambassador Sir Archibald Clark-Kerr and his Chilean wife, Tita. The writers judged Shanghai, its outer limits already claimed by the Japanese, 'more miserable than elsewhere'. Nevertheless, Auden and Isherwood, after the all traumas of war, chose to take 'afternoon holidays from their social conscience in a bath-house where you were erotically soaped and massaged by young men'.

On 12 June, they set sail from Shanghai onboard a Canadian Pacific liner named the *Empress of Asia*. This ship, as Isherwood was to comment upon, wryly, was set to call in at three ports in Japan (Kobe, Tokyo, Yokohama), before the writers were to continue their journey to London via Vancouver, Portal (North Dakota), Chicago and New York.

By the time they arrived in London on 17 July 1938, Auden had already decided he would emigrate to the United States, and Isherwood was to follow; their *Journey to a War* leading, in the end, to a kind of retreat, after witnessing its brutal reality in Asia.

Jane Austen Gets a Whiff of Sea Air (and Seaweed) in Worthing

Despite being a seafaring country, the British were surprisingly slow to take to the coast for leisure and pleasure. It was only after quack doctors began to tout sea water as a cure for gout in the late seventeenth century that the affluent unwell started to visit previously undistinguished fishing villages such as Scarborough in Yorkshire and Margate in Kent. 'Mad' King George III was the first British monarch to go to the seaside for his health, bathing at Weymouth in Dorset in 1789, and thanks to the patronage of his son George, the Prince Regent, the scrofulous Sussex coastal town of Brighthelmsea was re-born as Brighton, the pre-eminent marine watering place. Virtually simultaneously, the Romantics were making the ocean aesthetically 'sublime' and the sea a wonder to look out upon.

One writer who witnessed these extraordinary phenomena was Jane Austen (1775–1817), who not only dedicated her 1815 novel, *Emma*, perhaps somewhat archly, to 'His Royal Highness, The Prince Regent' but also began to write *Sanditon*, a pointed satire of the seaside boom, in the final months of her life. Abandoned on 18 March 1817 when she became too ill to continue (and not published in any form until 1925), this unfinished novel shows Austen still to be one of the keenest observers of human folly. More remarkably, given its author was terminally ill, one of its chief targets is hypochondria; her talons at their sharpest when pillorying the well-off, worried well having a high time indulging themselves with absurd marine cures.

Austen, as ever, was writing about what she knew. Following the unexpected decision in 1800 of her father to retire, Jane, her parents and her sister, Cassandra, were to live a largely peripatetic existence for much of the next decade. Nominally based in the inland spa town of Bath in Somerset, the Austens were also to spend time in the newly emerging coastal resorts of Sidmouth, Dawlish and Teignmouth in Devon, Charmouth and Lyme Regis in Dorset and most likely also went to Tenby and Barmouth in Wales. Some of these places and their landscapes were to creep into Austen's fictions, notably Lyme Regis in *Persuasion*, her last fully completed novel, published posthumously at the end of 1817. But it was a stay in the Sussex town of Worthing in the late summer and early autumn of 1805 that she channelled for *Sanditon*.

Worthing had been a fishing hamlet consisting, in the seaside historian J.A.R. Pimlott's pithy summation, 'of a few miserable cottages' when in 1798 it was graced by the presence of Princess Amelia, King George III's youngest daughter. Said to suffer with very delicate nerves and an invalid for much of her brief life, Amelia had been recently diagnosed with 'tuberculosis of the knee'. She was sent to Worthing to convalesce, her doctor suggesting it as a calmer alternative to the already racy Brighton.

By the time Austen arrived seven years later, Worthing had undergone a mini speculative building bonanza. Five plush new streets-cum-terraces –

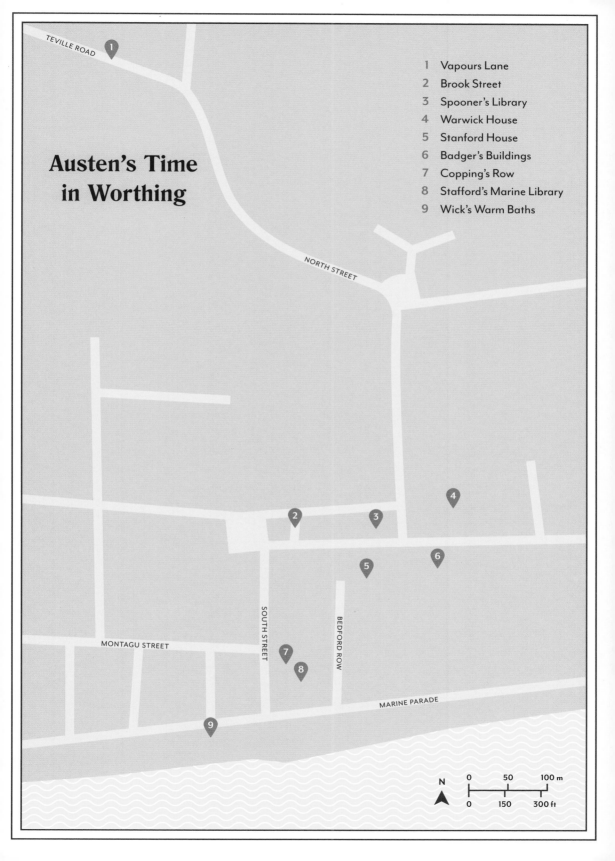

Bedford Row, Copping's Row, Brook Street (renamed South Place), Beach Row and Hertford Street, the last two long since lost but most of the others still standing in some form or other – were among the new additions to the town in the intervening period. But Worthing hadn't really advanced much as a resort and there were still only seven sparsely ranged buildings on what would become the front. A turnpike road from West Grinstead to Worthing had been completed in 1804, making the town far more accessible. But, as the local historian Antony Edwards has pointed out, in 1805 there were few shops, and still 'no market, no church, no theatre and no hotel'.

Three inns and Wick's Warm Baths were among Worthing's shoreside attractions. The latter Austen most likely frequented; her sister Cassandra most definitely did. There was nothing yet approaching a promenade. A new road along the shoreline to Lancing, replacing an earlier coastal path that had been washed away, was not to be built until 1807 (the same year the town's first hotel, the Steyne Hotel opened). The Esplanade, both a seafront promenade and a coastal defensive scheme, wouldn't be laid until the beginning of the 1820s.

Edwards records that the town retained a poor reputation for its marshy ground, fogs, bad air and smelly seaweed until improvements were made to its drainage. Revealingly, Edwards notes that the main road that trailed east to west at Worthing's northern end (today called Teville Road) was known in the nineteenth century as Vapours Lane. Austen was to comment acidly on these off-putting elements in her novel. Although in a sly act of misdirection, along with placing her fictional town of Sanditon nearer to Eastbourne, clearly intended to avoid immediate identification with the real Worthing, she gave these problems (a stagnant marsh, a ridge of putrefying seaweed, etc.) to another invented rival resort, Brinshore.

In Austen's day the grandest building in Worthing was Warwick House. Dating from 1789, perhaps slightly earlier, and finally demolished in 1896, this former residence of George Greville, 2nd Earl of Warwick, had been purchased by Edward Ogle in 1801. A wealthy London merchant at the forefront of promoting improvement schemes to hasten Worthing's transformation into a resort for the gentry and a place for genteel retirees, Ogle was to spend considerable sums of his immense fortune remaking his coastal property and its garden and grounds. If a little way inland, but with only a row of three cottages, known locally as Badger's Buildings, and an expanse of open ground between it and the shore, the house enjoyed uninterrupted sea views. Its position, nevertheless, did also leave it rather open to the elements. Ogle and his mansion were to appear, heavily embellished, in *Sanditon* as the desperate booster Mr Parker who lives in Trafalgar House.

Since Austen was in residence from the 18 September until at least 4 November 1805, and possibly even lingered on for Christmas, its likely she heard the news of Admiral Nelson's victory at the Battle of Trafalgar on 25 October that same year while in Worthing. In any case, in *Sanditon* Mr Parker is depicted as a hopeless trend chaser, confessing to regretting naming his house Trafalgar now that Waterloo is all the rage, and aiming to rectify this by erecting a new crescent in honour of Wellington's besting of Napoleon. Something not dissimilar would actually happen to at least one hostelry in Worthing, when what had been Marine Cottage in 1805 was enlarged and renamed the Wellington Inn in 1816.

Austen lodged in Stanford House, off what was to become Warwick Street, staying there with her mother, Cassandra and her friend Martha Lloyd, their household augmented for a while by Austen's brother Edward, his wife, Elizabeth, their daughter Fanny and her governess Mrs Sharpe. A pleasant white-

WORTHING, FROM THE BEACH.

▲ *Worthing, from the Beach, The Illustrated London News,*
25 August 1849.

stuccoed Georgian residence, Stanford House was then blessed with an open situation and sea views. Her other haunts in 1805 included St Mary's Church in the then-neighbouring inland village of Broadwater (which was to serve as Old Sanditon in the novel) and the town's two libraries: Spooner's Library in the Colonnade, almost directly opposite Stanford House and owned by Ogle, and Stafford's Marine Library in Marine Place, which also served as the town's post office. These libraries also sold novelty goods and toys and staged evenings of polite entertainments that were suitable enough for respectable ladies to attend, and chiefly centred, seemingly, around raffles. Austen, we know from Fanny's diary, was to scoop a prize of seven shillings at one draw held on the night of 19 September, most probably in Spooner's Library.

Austen, as far we know, never visited Worthing again. *Sanditon*, if only a fragment, would probably lead most readers to assume the novelist had no wish ever to go back there. But perhaps the finest satires are conceived as acts of love, and she wrote the novel partially in mourning for the more innocent, quieter watering place she visited in 1805. A resort that by 1817, she knew full well would already have altered beyond recognition.

◀ The Victorian pier in
Worthing, England.

James Baldwin Falls for Paris in the Fall

Born in the Harlem neighbourhood of New York to a single mother, who never disclosed the identity of his father and later married a tyrannical Baptist preacher before going on to bear eight more children, James Baldwin (1924–1987) maintained that he 'had to become a writer or perish'. Black and gay in an era of segregation and when homosexuality was illegal and gay men and lesbians were purged from government jobs and the military as security risks, Baldwin would have to leave America to achieve his ambition. In fact, the author of *Giovanni's Room* was to spend the majority of his writing life outside the United States, residing mostly in Turkey between 1961 and 1971 and after that spending the bulk of his final years in the village of Saint-Paul-de-Vence in Provence in the south of France. But it was his first excursion outside America and to Paris in 1948 that was, unarguably, the most formative.

As Baldwin was often at pains to point out, he not did especially wish to leave his homeland; the departure was an act of desperation. He felt driven out by racism, poverty and homophobia. A close friend had committed suicide by jumping in the Harlem River, and he feared he might end up doing something similar. The last straw was finding himself refused service on the grounds of his colour in a restaurant in Trenton, New Jersey.

The remains of a grant awarded to Baldwin by the Rosenwald Fellowship Program for a never-realized project documenting shorefront churches in Harlem with his friend, the photographer Theodore Pelatowski, paid for a one-way aeroplane ticket. He flew from New York to Paris on 11 November 1948 with just $40 in his pocket and reams of his uncompleted manuscripts and a few books and clothes stuffed into a duffle bag. If his departure was low-key and hasty (he only informed his mother and siblings of the plan on the evening of his flight), news of his arrival in France had been conveyed via mutual friends to a distinguished coterie of American expats, including some old Harlem and Greenwich Village acquaintances, who were eager see him in Paris.

Among them were Asa Benveniste and George Solomos (whose pen name was Themistocles Hoetis), two recent blow-ins from the United States who were on the brink of starting *Zero*, a new literary magazine. The day Baldwin arrived, they'd been soliciting potential contributions from the French philosopher Jean-Paul Sartre and the Black American novelist Richard Wright (Baldwin's one-time mentor) over lunch in Les Deux Magots, the café on Saint-Germain-des-Prés frequented in its heyday by everyone from Ernest Hemingway to Simone de Beauvoir. Baldwin, who'd travelled in 'the absolute certainty of being dashed to death on the vindictive tooth of the Eiffel Tower', found instead a small welcoming committee, headed by Benveniste (who he'd not previously met), waiting for him at the Gare des Invalides railway station. He was then promptly escorted straight to Les Deux Magots, where he was

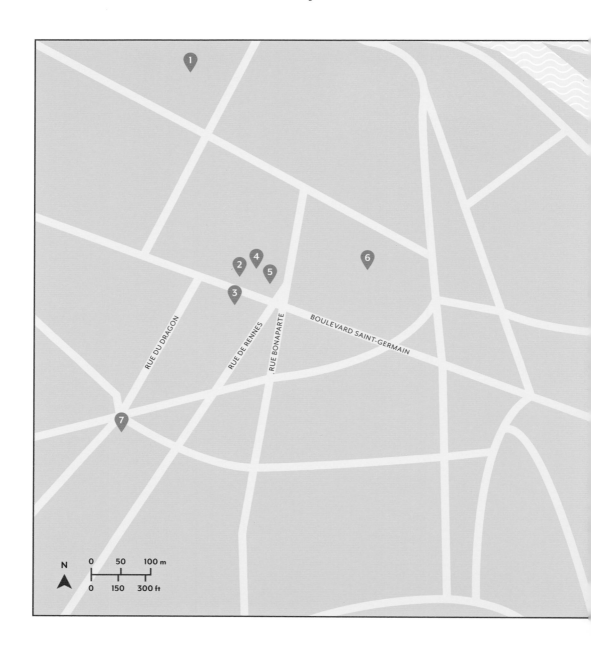

RUE DU DRAGON

RUE DE RENNES

RUE BONAPARTE

BOULEVARD SAINT-GERMAIN

N

| 0 | 50 | 100 m |
| 0 | 150 | 300 ft |

◀ PREVIOUS PAGE View over
the rooftops, Paris.

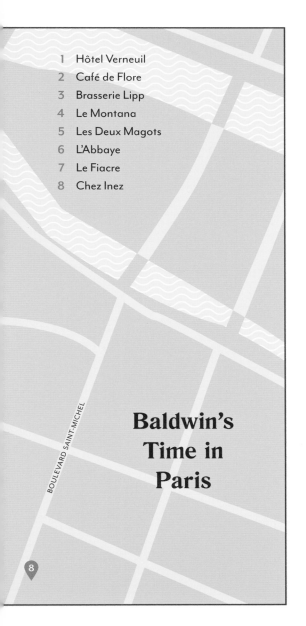

1 Hôtel Verneuil
2 Café de Flore
3 Brasserie Lipp
4 Le Montana
5 Les Deux Magots
6 L'Abbaye
7 Le Fiacre
8 Chez Inez

BOULEVARD SAINT-MICHEL

Baldwin's Time in Paris

introduced to Solomos and reunited with Wright, who helped his former protégé find a cheap room at the Hôtel de Rome on the boulevard Saint-Michel.

Thanks to another old friend from New York, Priscilla Broughton, Baldwin would soon move to a no-less rundown but rather more convivial establishment nearby on the rue de Verneuil. The Hôtel Verneuil was run by a Corsican family and presided over by the clan's formidable matriarch, Madame Dumont. Reasonable about rent and generally tolerant about unorthodox hours and, indeed, lifestyles, she held soirées where invitations were not infrequently extended to the hotel's guests. It says much about her compassionate nature that Dumont nursed Baldwin back to health when he fell ill in the bitter winter of January 1949, an act of kindness he never forgot.

Through Broughton, Baldwin was introduced to another Verneuil resident, Mary Keen, an English trade union activist, whose suite served as a meeting-house-cum-canteen for a plethora of other expat waifs and strays in the vicinity. One woman in this circle who Baldwin was to become especially close to was the boyish Norwegian journalist Gidske Anderson, who wrote for a socialist paper in Oslo; the pair were inseparable for a time in Paris.

Baldwin had come to France to write. Since the rooms in the Verneuil were unheated, he would diligently haul himself and his notebooks and a fountain pen off to Les Deux Magots or, more often, to the upstairs room of Café de Flore, the Magots's main rival on the corner of boulevard Saint-Germain and rue

Saint-Benoît. Dosing himself with coffee throughout the day, he would scribble away into the evening.

Another of Baldwin's daytime haunts was the Brasserie Lipp, directly across the street from the Flore. It was here that Baldwin had an altercation with Wright after the publication of his first piece in *Zero*, 'Everybody's Protest Novel' – an article that Wright took, not unreasonably, as an attack on his own civil rights-driven output and he accused the younger writer of betraying African-Americans as a whole. It was a charge that Baldwin fiercely denied. Their relationship was severely strained after this incident, but it did survive.

Normally after leaving the cafés, Baldwin and his companions would gravitate to neighbourhood bars and nightclubs to pursue their drinking in earnest. On occasion such sessions continued into the small hours and could involve detours to French-Algerian eateries in Le Pigalle to smoke hashish and end with breakfast in one of the working men's cafés beside the markets at Les Halles. More generally, Baldwin's main ports of call were Le Montana, a bar on the rue Saint-Benoît; L'Abbaye on the rue Jacob, which was a Left Bank folk and blues club run by the American actor Gordon Heath; and Chez Inez, a jazz joint and soul food restaurant founded by Inez Cavanaugh, a Chicagoan who'd once acted as a secretary to the Harlem Renaissance poet Langston Hughes. It was in the latter venue that a stone-broke Baldwin once sang for his supper, literally; belting out Ira Gershwin's 'The Man I Love' in exchange for a plate of fried chicken.

▲ Inez Cavanaugh sings in her club, Chez Inez, Saint-Germain-des-Prés, Paris, 1949.

▶ The terrace of Café de Flore, Paris, June 1948.

When it came to seeking male companionship, however, La Reine Blanche, on the south side of the boulevard Saint-Germain, and its more upmarket neighbour, Le Fiacre, which would later serve as the model for Guillaume's bar in *Giovanni's Room*, were among the few openly gay bars in Paris during Baldwin's first stint in the city. It was in La Reine Blanche that Baldwin was to meet Lucien Happersberger, the Swiss artist he'd call the love of his life.

If Baldwin was producing articles and essays, his novel, a semi-autobiographical fiction about a young boy growing up in Harlem in the 1930s with a Pentecostal preacher for a father, still stubbornly refused to be finished. Concerned about his lover's lack of progress on the book in Paris, Happersberger proposed that they decamp to his family's cabin in Loèche-les-Bains (Leukerbad) in Switzerland, where Baldwin might write with fewer distractions. And indeed it was there that over three months in the winter of 1951–2 he completed *Go Tell It On the Mountain*. Interest from an American publisher and a loan from the actor Marlon Brando would carry Baldwin, briefly, back to America. But the pattern for a nomadic transatlantic existence had been set in motion.

Bashō Takes the Narrow Road to the Deep North

Poets tend to be ambulant creatures, almost preternaturally disposed to wandering. Yet few can claim to have put quite so much legwork into their output as the Japanese versifier Matsuo Kinsaku (1644–1694), better known as Bashō. One of the foremost masters of the haiku, Bashō wrote at least a thousand of these short-form poems, along with organizing several anthologies of verse. However, his most highly regarded works remain a sequence of travel sketches describing the places he visited on his restless peregrinations around Japan, written in a hybrid form called *haibun* that combines spare descriptive prose and haiku to near transcendent effect. The finest of these poetic narratives, widely acclaimed as one of the greatest books in classical Japanese literature, is an account of his journey into the remote northern provinces of Japan, *Oku no Hosomichi*, most commonly translated in English as 'The Narrow Road to the Deep North'.

Bashō is believed to have been born in Ueno in Iga Province, about 48 kilometres/30 miles south-east of Kyoto. His father, Matsuo Yozaemon, was a samurai who supported his family by farming. At the age of twelve and following his father's death, Bashō was sent into the service of Todo Yoshitada, a young relative of the local feudal lord. Despite their differences in status, the two boys struck up a firm

friendship and studied poetry and began writing haikus together. Following Yoshitada's premature death in 1666, Bashō left Ueno and headed for Kyoto.

By 1672, Bashō was in Tokyo (then Edo) and already carving out a reputation as one of the city's most formidable poets and attracting a slew of acolytes and admirers. Nevertheless, the news of his mother's death in 1683 was to set him off in new directions, geographically and creatively. The following August he undertook a monkish pilgrimage to his native region. Accompanied by Chiri, a young man who kindly assumed the position of a servant, and following the example of an ancient Chinese priest by packing no provisions, Bashō journeyed for a month to reach his mother's home. The fruit of this voyage was to be the first of his poetic travelogues, *The Records of a Weather-exposed Skeleton*. This book was to set the pattern for his mature style, with wayfaring now becoming a way of life for Bashō. As he would write in *The Records of a Travel-worn Satchel*:

> First Winter rain –
> I plod on,
> Traveller, my name.

But as Nobuyuki Yuasa, one of Bashō's first English translators, was at pains to point out, travel

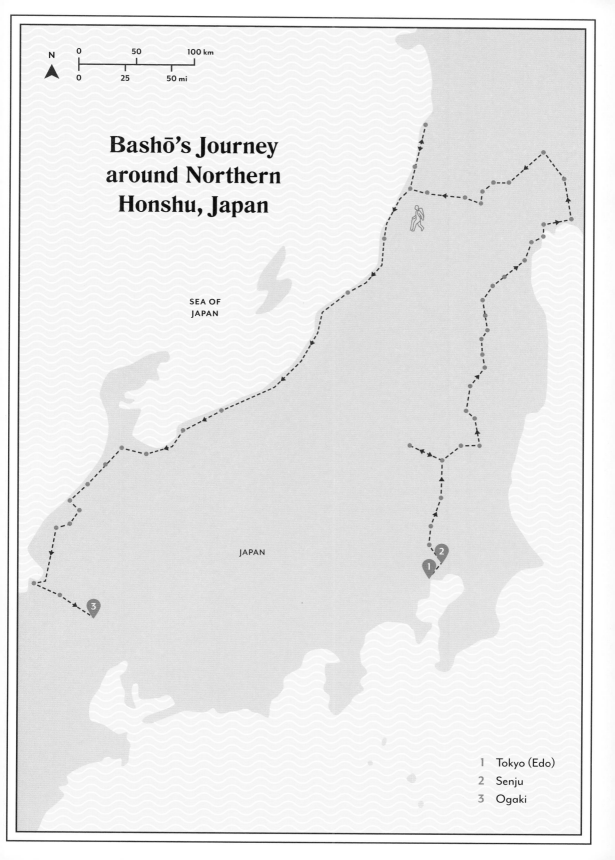

Bashō's Journey around Northern Honshu, Japan

N

0   50   100 km
0 25   50 mi

SEA OF JAPAN

JAPAN

1 Tokyo (Edo)
2 Senju
3 Ogaki

'in his day had to be made under very precarious conditions ... few people, if any, thought of taking to the road merely for pleasure or pastime'.

Bashō himself hints at the potential for danger in his introduction to *The Narrow Road to the Deep North*, writing,

This year, the second year of Genroku, I have decided to make a long walking trip to the distant provinces of the far north. Though the hardships of the journey will pile up snowy hairs on my head, I will see with my own eyes places of which I have only heard – I cannot even be certain that I will return alive.

That he seriously believed this could be his final journey is possibly indicated by the poet's decision to sell his home ahead of his departure on 16 May 1689. He was forty-five years of age at this time and already in slightly frail health. The choice to venture beyond the Shirakawa barrier, a mythic, here-be-dragons crossing point between the refined society of Tokyo and the untamed northern hinterlands would have struck some of his disciples as near suicidal.

With the cherry blossoms in bloom, a small band of his followers accompanied him on the short boat trip up the Sumida River from Tokyo to Senju, where Bashō and his friend Kawai Sora made for the Ōshūkaidō, a highway that formed part of the Great North Road. They were to follow its course through the coastal plain and up into the remote rural province of Oshu for six weeks. Turning inland, they entered country where, according to Bashō, the forests were so thick that they 'couldn't hear one bird cry, and under the trees it was so dark that it was like walking at midnight'. Trekking deep into the northern mountains, they were to spend a week with the yamabushi, a near-mythic order of hermit priests whose reclusiveness far exceeded even Basho's own desire for peace and solitude.

This idyllic sojourn was to be followed by one of the most arduous stages of their journey, a concluding tramp back down Japan's western coast on the Hokurikudō highway to the town of Ogaki, which they reached on 18 October 1689. In *The Narrow Road to the Deep North* Bashō wraps up his narrative at this point. But it was to be a further two years before he found his way back to Tokyo, during which period the poet continued to wander, seeking and receiving hospitality from friends and disciples around Kyoto and elsewhere.

Having eventually committed his account of these northerly ambles to paper, Bashō became anxious to travel again, this time setting his sights on the south of Japan. Leaving Tokyo in the spring, he was in Osaka by the autumn. There he seems to have suffered an attack of dysentery, dying four days later on 12 October 1694. Among his last acts, he penned a poem entitled 'Sick in Bed', in which he regretted having been 'Seized with a disease' when only 'Halfway on the Road' – his wanderlust undiminished right up until the end.

▶ Matsushima Bay, Tohoku, Japan.

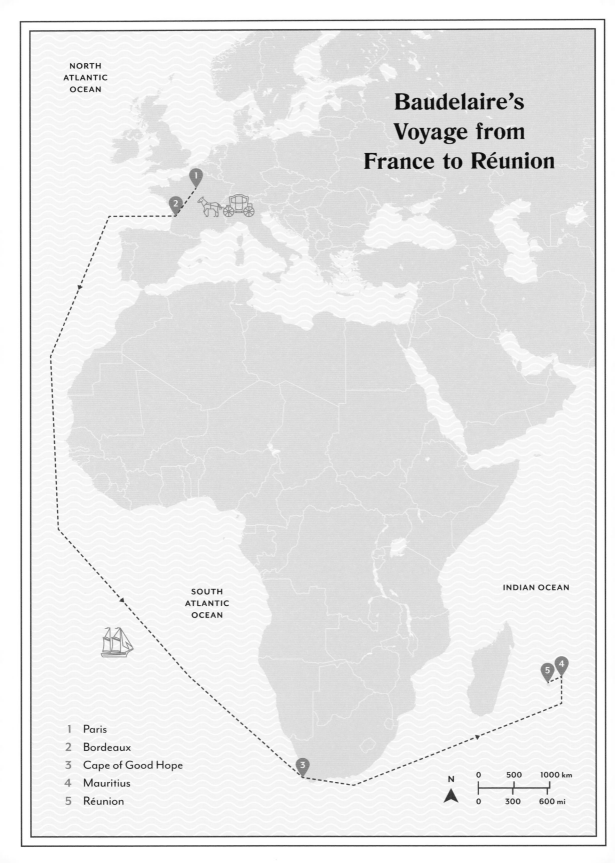

NORTH
ATLANTIC
OCEAN

Baudelaire's
Voyage from
France to Réunion

SOUTH
ATLANTIC
OCEAN

INDIAN OCEAN

1 Paris
2 Bordeaux
3 Cape of Good Hope
4 Mauritius
5 Réunion

N

0	500	1000 km
0	300	600 mi

Charles Baudelaire Fails to Make It to India

Two years after leaving the Lycée Louis-le-Grand in Paris, where he'd been a reluctant student of that most respectable of subjects, law, Charles Baudelaire (1821–1867) was leading a life so debauched that his family hatched a plan to set him on the straight and narrow. He would, of course, go on to become one of the greatest and most influential French poets of the nineteenth century, and an essayist who shaped contemporary literary thought and tastes. But in 1841, he was a callow, if budding, literary lion who had run up debts of over 2,000 francs, fallen madly in love with a strumpet and, as his mother later put it, 'attached himself to bohemians of the worst sort, to whom he was drawn by a desire to satisfy his curiosity concerning the mysterious haunts of vice in Paris'.

At a family conference convened in Neuilly, a suburb of Paris, with a notary present, Baudelaire's stepfather, General Aupick, mother and brother agreed that the only thing for it was to dispatch the errant youth to India, where – removed from the temptations of Paris and his unsavoury companions – he might come to his senses and see the error of his ways. Legend has it that on receiving the news of his fate from his stepfather, Baudelaire attempted to strangle Aupick. But more recent biographers discount this story, and if not exactly thrilled by the

idea to begin with, it has been suggested he did welcome the opportunity to travel to the East at least, which had long held a certain romantic fascination to the poet for its perceived exoticism.

That Baudelaire would be required to undertake a lengthy ocean voyage to reach the subcontinent was a crucial element in the choice of destination over possible alternative schemes to see him placed in a dull part of Germany or Belgium. Aupick, like Baudelaire's mother, was an orphan, who at four had been adopted by the magistrate and harbour-master at the Channel port of Gravelines, on the coast of northern France. While his own distinguished military career was carved in the field and in the Franco-Spanish War, he retained a deep love of ships and the sea from his childhood and genuinely believed that time on a boat would be beneficial to his stepson.

Before all that, however, Baudelaire had to undertake the five-day journey from Paris to Bordeaux, where his ship, the *Paquebot-des-Mers-du-Sud*, was waiting for him. Ultimately bound for Kolkata (then Calcutta), the *Mers-du-Sud* was to leave Bordeaux on 9 June 1841, slipping along the Gironde estuary and out into the North Atlantic. Baudelaire had been entrusted into the care of the vessel's commander, Captain Saliz. The shipmaster received a stipend from Aupick to keep an eye on his stepson and held the poet's passage money under lock and key to ensure he didn't squander any of it before reaching India. Any initial thrill Baudelaire might have felt striding around on the deck and imagining himself as a nautical adventurer rapidly wore off. The other passengers, mostly commercial types or army officers, bored him rigid with their platitudinous observations about the weather.

The long voyage on board this tiny ship was claustrophobic, uncomfortable and pretty monotonous. But just at a point when the tedium threatened to overwhelm him, the ship was caught up in a typhoon off the Cape of Good Hope, the justly feared rocky headland on the Atlantic coast of the Cape Peninsula in South Africa, and the vessel nearly sunk. Such was the damage that the *Mers-du-Sud* was forced to stop in Mauritius for two weeks for repairs, leaving Baudelaire free to explore this

cosmopolitan island in the Indian Ocean. Here he appears to have become acquainted with a few of the French expat community, among them the solicitor Autard de Bragard, his beautiful wife and their young daughter. Madame de Bragard was subsequently to enjoy posthumous fame as the inspiration for 'To a Creole Lady', a sonnet that featured in Baudelaire's most famous collection, *The Flowers of Evil*.

When the time came for his ship to depart, however, Baudelaire told Saliz in no uncertain terms that he was through with the whole idea of India and would go no further. Saliz prevailed upon the poet at least to continue on to Réunion (then Bourbon Island), just a day's sail away, where the naval man would endeavour to find the poet a ship heading back to France. True to his word, Saliz arranged for Baudelaire to join the *Alcide*, a cargo ship then docked at Saint-Denis, the capital of Réunion. If the

homesick poet was hoping for a speedy return to Paris, however, he was to be disappointed; the *Alcide* was undergoing a lengthy re-fit, and Baudelaire, who had arrived on Réunion on 9 September, had to wait until 4 November before the boat set sail.

The homeward voyage was marginally more interesting but no more comfortable, as the *Alcide* was an even smaller vessel than the *Mers-du-Sud*. The ship called in on Cape Town for a couple of days and Baudelaire enjoyed looking around the town, taking an interest in its colonial architecture and noting, rather disdainfully, the number of sheep farms, and the woolly aroma of the place.

From South Africa, the ship headed up the western coast of Africa, across the Gulf of Guinea and onwards into the North Atlantic, finally landing at Bordeaux in the second week of February 1842. Within two months of returning home, Baudelaire would come into his

majority, allowing him the financial freedom to live as he pleased (as long as the money lasted).

Unfortunately for his mother and stepfather, Baudelaire's commitment to poetic fame and the dissolute life was utterly undiminished by his time at sea. While the voyage stripped him of any desire to step foot on a ship again, the trip would, nevertheless, furnish Baudelaire with material throughout his career. The return leg, in particular, would be spun as a great adventure, though one that the poet felt no need to repeat, with the fleshpots and viperous literary salons never more than a saunter away from him in Paris after all.

▼ Saint-Denis docks, Réunion. Illustration by Évremonde de Bérard, 1862.

▶ NEXT PAGE Le Morne Brabant, Mauritius.

Elizabeth Bishop Is Bowled Over by Brazil

In the autumn of 1951, the American poet Elizabeth Bishop (1911–1979) was at something of a crossroads in her life. An alcoholic afflicted by bouts of anxiety and depression who sought help for her addiction and mental health problems through psychoanalysis, she had been living a fairly rootless existence since giving up her home in Key West, Florida in 1946. But the award of the first Lucy Martin Donnelly Fellowship from Bryn Mawr College in Pennsylvania supplied Bishop with the opportunity to get some distance from North America. Bishop mapped out an ambitious itinerary for a lengthy tour of South America, including stops at Rio de Janeiro in Brazil, Buenos Aires and Montevideo in Argentina and Punta Arenas in Chile, before moving on to Peru and Ecuador.

Set to leave on the Norwegian merchant ship MS *Bowplate* on 26 October 1951, her departure was delayed by a dock strike until 10 November. The hold-up was, in a sense, to be a prelude to her whole excursion, which would be stalled by circumstances (some awful, some wonderful) in Brazil, where she would, for the most part, make her home for the next seventeen years.

Bound for the Brazilian city of Santos, the *Bowplate* was carrying a large cargo of jeeps and combines and just nine passengers, including Bishop herself. Of her fellow voyagers only one, a Miss Breen, interested the poet. An ex-police officer and retired head of a women's prison in Detroit,

Michigan, Breen was a striking woman, nearly 1.75 metres/6 feet tall with 'large blue eyes and bluish waved hair', as Bishop later recounted in letters to friends. With an almost inexhaustible supply of stories about violent crime, she proved pleasant company for the duration of a sluggish course across the Atlantic; their ship, as a jobbing freighter, travelling at around half the speed of a Cunard passenger liner.

Once the women landed at Santos, Breen was met by two old friends who were to give Bishop a lift in their car to São Paulo, about 80 kilometres/50 miles inland. This first encounter with Brazil was to be memorialized in verse in 'Arrival at Santos', one of the first poems she wrote in the country, subsequently published in the *New Yorker* magazine and reprinted in her Pulitzer prize-winning *Poems: North & South – A Cold Spring*. That volume was to boast two other early Brazilian poems: 'The Mountain' and 'The Shampoo'. The latter, which described the tender act of washing a dear friend's hair in a tin basin, had been rejected by both the *New Yorker* and *Poetry*, to which Bishop was also a valued contributor. Although the friend's gender is never stated, the poem was written as a veiled tribute to her new Brazilian lover, the wealthy socialite and property developer Lota de Macedo Soares. Bishop's biographer Thomas Travisano is not alone in concluding that these magazines were most likely uncomfortable with the poem's underlying homoeroticism.

Bishop had previously met Soares when the Brazilian visited New York in 1942. A great champion of the poet's verse ever since then, and something of a mover and shaker in artistic and aristocratic circles in Brazil, Soares was one of the few people that Bishop had arranged to see in Rio de Janeiro ahead of her trip. Another was Pearl Kazin, the American editor, writer and critic and one-time lover of Dylan Thomas, who'd only recently moved to Brazil with her photographer husband Victor Kraft. Bishop was to reach Rio de Janeiro on 30 November 1951, having taken a train there from São Paulo, and was greeted at the station by Kazin and Mary Morse, Soares's Bostonion factotum, business associate and former romantic partner.

The poet was soon installed in Soares's palatial penthouse apartment at rua Antonio Vieira 5 in the affluent district of Leme, with a maid to attend to her needs and an unparalleled vista of the city and the Copacabana Beach from its eleventh-floor balcony. Soares didn't neglect her guest, taking it upon herself to escort the poet on two days of sightseeing around the Brazilian capital and inviting Bishop to come and see the *fazenda*, or summer house, she was building for herself with the young Brazilian modernist architect Sérgio Bernardes out in the Serra dos Órgãos mountains to the west of the capital. This property at Samambaia, just beyond the ancient imperial city of Petrópolis, was then very much a work in progress. Reaching it involved a 90-minute drive through increasingly vertiginous terrain in Soares's Land Rover.

Both Bishop's grandfather and father had been involved in the building trade and there was clearly something about Soares's endeavours at this scenic outpost that touched the poet. Nevertheless, she

5

6

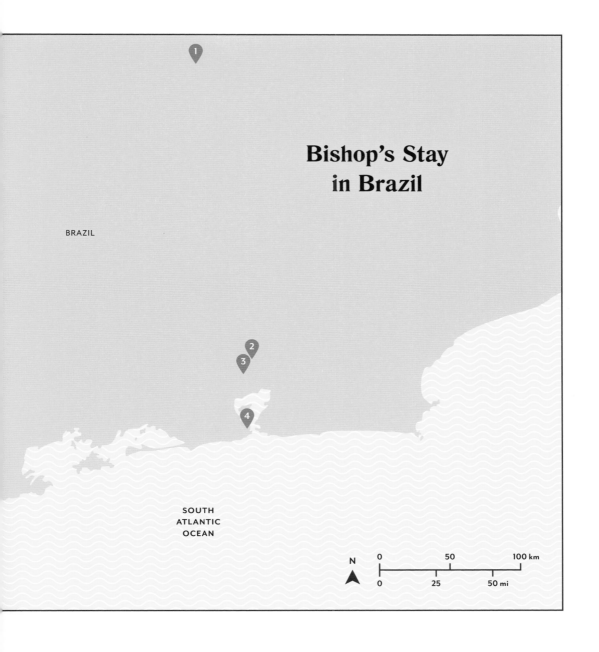

Bishop's Stay
in Brazil

BRAZIL

SOUTH
ATLANTIC
OCEAN

N

| 0 | | 50 | | 100 km |
| 0 | 25 | | 50 mi | |

◀ PREVIOUS PAGE Serra dos
Órgãos National Park, Brazil.

had every intention of continuing her travels until she suffered an appalling reaction to eating the fruit of a cashew tree. Confined to the hospital in Petrópolis and afterwards forced to recuperate at Samambaia, she had to miss her scheduled connection to Tierra del Fuego. Soares, who'd cared for Bishop throughout this sickness, now invited the poet to stay on with her in Brazil, an offer the American accepted, their romance blossoming amid the mountain scenery and the wealthier woman's promise to build a studio for the writer to work in beside the main house at Samambaia.

When forced to explain her decision to relocate to Brazil to disbelieving literary associates in the United States, Bishop would simply tell them, 'I am here because the one I love is here.' But their relationship was often far from easy. Bishop's hospitalization after heavy drinking following her use

of a new drug for asthma and Soares's acceptance of what turned out to be a fraught government job to (successfully) turn a rubbish dump in Rio de Janeiro into a public park (Flamengo Park), which forced the couple to live more constantly in the Leme apartment, were among the factors that gradually drove a wedge between them. The political situation in Brazil itself, after a military coup in 1964, further added to their growing estrangement.

While in Brazil, Bishop learned Portuguese and became a formidable translator of Brazilian prose and verse into English (if always a reluctant speaker of the language in public). After reading *Minha Vida de Menina* ('My Life As a Young Girl'), a popular account of an impoverished upbringing in the city of Diamantina in the 1890s by Alice Brandt, Bishop was inspired to translate Brandt's book (published in 1957 as *The Diary of 'Helena Morley'*), which in turn

spurred on her own writing about her formative years
in the Canadian province of Nova Scotia.

Bishop was to produce a monograph on Brazil
and its history for Life World Library and established
a second home in the country, Casa Mariana, out
in Ouro Preto, a town in the Serra do Espinhaço
mountains of eastern Brazil. It was here that Bishop
returned in the wake of Soares's death in September
1967, her lover taking an overdose of Nembutal
shortly after arriving at the poet's flat in New York.
Bishop would continue to visit Brazil in the remaining
decade of her life, but after 1968, it would cease
to be her home. Nevertheless its importance to her
poetic output is inestimable. *Questions of Travel*,
her collection of verse from 1965, was a landmark
work in examining the nature of a writer and their
relationship to place.

◄ Lota de Macedo Soares's house, Samambaia, Brazil.

▲ Ouro Preto, Brazil.

Heinrich Böll Is Enchanted by the Emerald Isle

Born into a liberal Catholic family in Cologne, Germany, Heinrich Böll (1917–1985) was a fearless examiner of his nation's recent past and a prober of the scars left by the Second World War. Although a pacifist and opponent of the Nazis, he was drafted into the Wehrmacht in 1939, suffering, as he once mordantly commented, the 'frightful fate of being a soldier and having to wish that the war might be lost'. Sent to the Russian and French fronts, he was wounded four times, and after deserting was captured and held in an American prisoner-of-war camp. Enrolling at the University of Cologne after the war, he was to drop out to concentrate on writing fiction. Böll's early stories, the first of which was published in 1947, and his propulsive and astonishingly economical debut novel, *The Train Was on Time*, which followed two years later, drew closely on his wartime experiences and presented determinedly anti-heroic accounts of soldiering. Castigated by certain sections of the German press for writing what was denounced as *Trümmerliteratur* ('rubble literature'), Böll was awarded the Nobel Prize for Literature in 1972.

Back in 1954, however, and following a short trip to England, Böll caught a steamer from Liverpool to Dublin. Almost from the instant he stepped on the boat and found himself in the company of 'the only people in Europe that never set out to conquer', he was beguiled. Crossing Ireland by train and bus from Dublin to Westport and on to Mayo, he observed the Irish at work, rest and play; noting the prodigious quantity of tea they drank ('enough tea to fill a small swimming pool must flow down every Irish throat every year') and their refreshingly relaxed attitude to time-keeping ('When God made time, the Irish say, He made plenty of it.'). Illustrating the latter point, Böll was to record that at the picture house in Keel, a village on the island of Achill off the north-west coast of Ireland, the movies would only begin once the priests arrived, regardless of what time was advertised in the programme. Böll also admired a certain willingness among Irish people to put a gloss on adversity. As he was to write:

> When something happens to you in Germany, when you miss a train, break a leg, go bankrupt, we say: It couldn't have been any worse; whatever happens is always the worst. With the Irish it is almost the opposite: if you break a leg, miss a train, go bankrupt, they say: It could be worse; instead of a leg you could have broken your neck, instead of a train you could have missed Heaven.

Böll would return to Ireland the following couple of summers, eventually buying a house on Achill in 1958, which he visited annually from thereon until 1973.

Ireland had remained neutral during the Second World War, and its towns and cities had therefore been spared the bombing raids that had laid waste to the likes of his native Cologne. But poverty and the lack of work meant many of the younger generation were forced to emigrate in the 1950s and 1960s, leaving some rural villages completely abandoned, as Böll was to document in *Irish Journal*. This impressionistic work began life as a series of articles about Ireland for the *Frankfurter Allgemeine Zeitung*. Published in Germany in 1957, the book triggered a wave of tourism to the country from his homeland. As the Irish writer Fintan O'Toole has noted, it was ironic that as 'mass emigration reached critical levels' Böll reinvented Ireland 'not as a place to escape from but as a place to escape to' – for West Germans, at least.

This development wasn't entirely welcomed by Böll. Nor did he much like the pace of change in Ireland itself; the disappearance of nuns from newspapers and the arrival of 'The Pill' he found especially concerning. Though he always conceded that for the Irish themselves things probably had improved. After 1973, he ceased his annual holidays there, only returning to Achill once a decade later, just two years before his death in 1985. His former home, surrounded by peat bogs and with views of the Atlantic, which would carry away so many Irishmen and women to new lives in America, today is preserved as a writer's retreat.

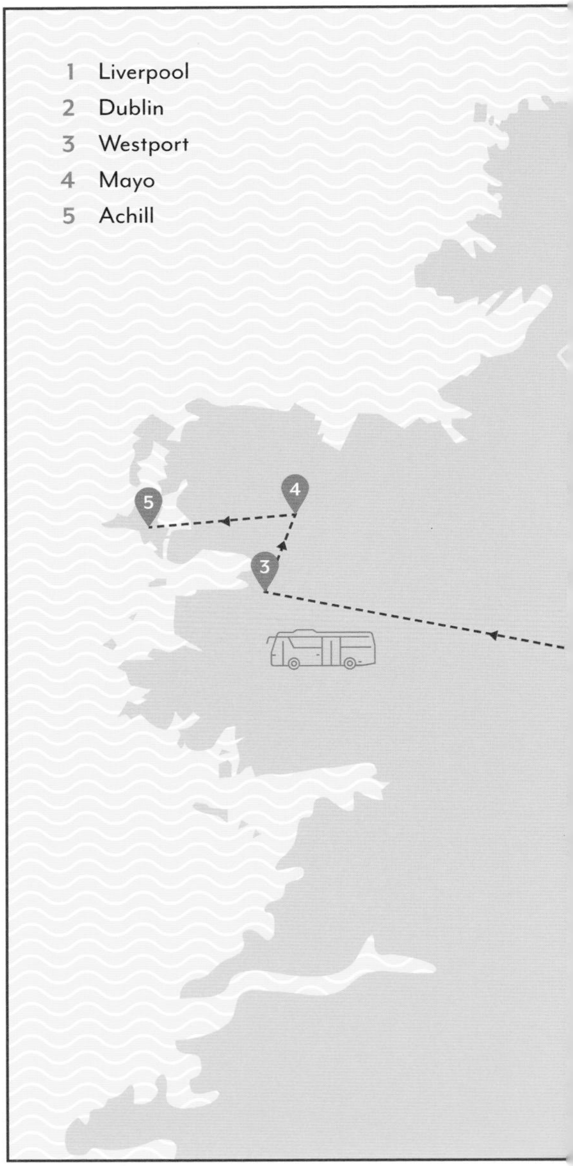

1 Liverpool
2 Dublin
3 Westport
4 Mayo
5 Achill

◀ PREVIOUS PAGE Achill Island, Ireland.

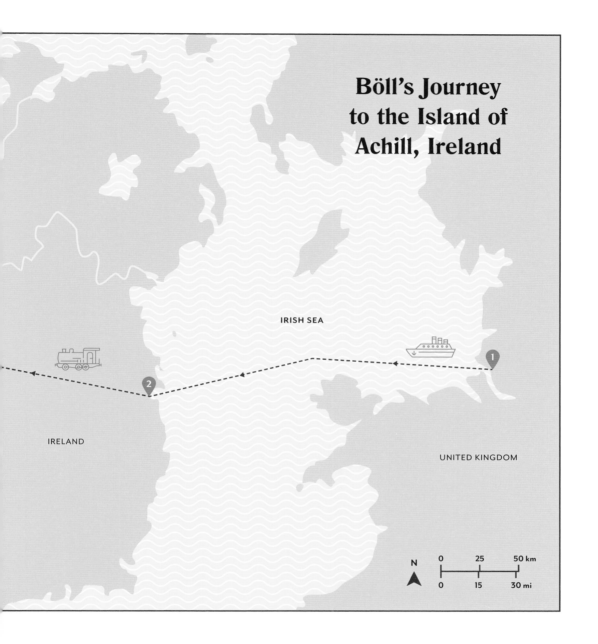

Böll's Journey
to the Island of
Achill, Ireland

IRISH SEA

IRELAND

UNITED KINGDOM

N

| 0 | 25 | 50 km |
| 0 | 15 | 30 mi |

Lewis Carroll Finds Another Wonderland in Russia

The mathematician, academic and author Charles Lutwidge Dodgson (1832–1898) is perhaps better known by his pen name of Lewis Carroll. He was a deeply religious man and was heavily involved in the Anglican theological debates of the day. The son of a Church of England parson, he had been destined for the church himself and was ordained as a deacon in 1861. But constitutionally ill-suited to parochial work, he opted to stay in academia, taking a post as a lecturer in mathematics at Christ Church, Oxford. Undergraduates, on first discovering that Carroll and Dodgson were one and the same, are said to have been utterly incredulous that their dry-as-dust tutor could ever have written anything as amusing as *Alice's Adventures in Wonderland*.

On 4 July 1867, two years to the day after Miss Alice Liddell had received the first presentation copy of *Alice's Adventures in Wonderland*, Carroll and his friend and fellow Oxford university don, the theologian Dr Henry Liddon, agreed to go to Russia together over the summer vacation. The purpose of their visit was a semi-official mission to build bridges with the Eastern Orthodox Church.

The pair sailed from Dover to Calais on 13 July, and made their way via Brussels, Cologne, Berlin (where they visited the most gorgeous synagogue), Gdańsk (Danzig) and Kaliningrad (Königsberg) to St Petersburg, which they reached by train on 27 July. Carroll found the capital of the Russian Empire full of wonder and novelty. The English academics spent several days exploring the city and its environs. Carroll was especially taken with its wide streets, teeming with life and the 'jabber of the natives', its 'gigantic churches, with their domes painted blue and covered with gold stars' and 'a fine equestrian statue of Peter the Great near the Admiralty'. There was also an excursion by steamer 32 kilometres/20 miles 'down the tideless, saltless Gulf of Finland' to the imperial palaces and grounds at Peterhof, whose gardens the mathematician thought eclipsed those of Sanssouci, Frederick the Great's palace at Potsdam, Germany.

But it was Moscow, where they went next by rail on 2 August (paying 2 roubles extra for sleeping-tickets), that turned their heads. Describing their first day there, Carroll summed up the city as a giddy whirl, one that seemed to distort the normal rules of perspective, writing:

> We gave five or six hours to a stroll through this wonderful city, a city of white houses and green roofs, of conical towers that rise one out of another like a foreshortened telescope; of bulging gilded domes, in which you see, as in a looking-glass, distorted pictures of the city; of churches

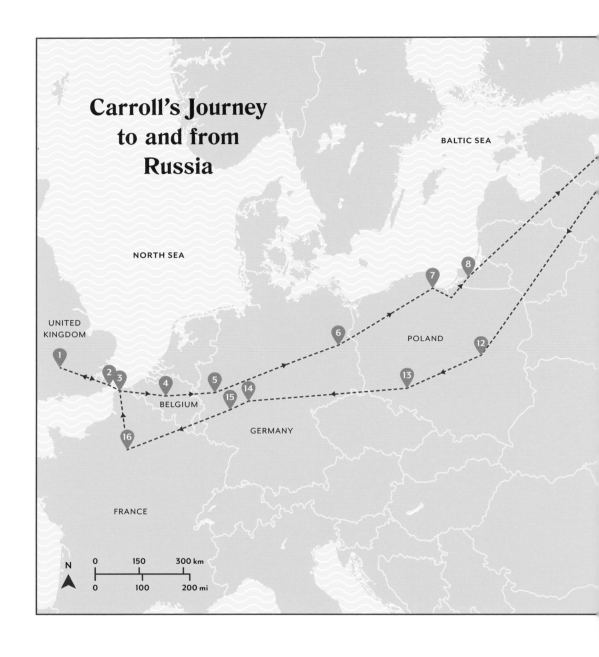

Carroll's Journey
to and from
Russia

BALTIC SEA

NORTH SEA

UNITED
KINGDOM

POLAND

BELGIUM

GERMANY

FRANCE

N

| 0 | 150 | 300 km |
| 0 | 100 | 200 mi |

◀ PREVIOUS PAGE St Basil's
Cathedral, Moscow.

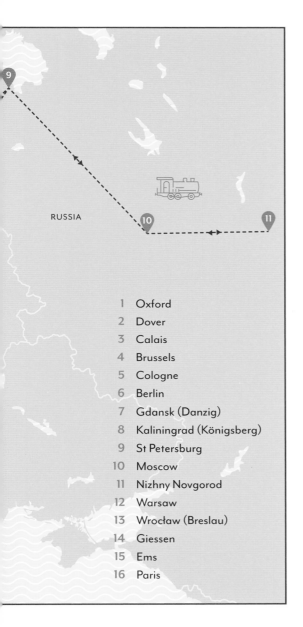

RUSSIA

1 Oxford
2 Dover
3 Calais
4 Brussels
5 Cologne
6 Berlin
7 Gdansk (Danzig)
8 Kaliningrad (Königsberg)
9 St Petersburg
10 Moscow
11 Nizhny Novgorod
12 Warsaw
13 Wrocław (Breslau)
14 Giessen
15 Ems
16 Paris

which look, outside, like bunches of variegated cactus (some branches crowned with green prickly buds, others with blue, and others with red and white) and which, inside, are hung all round with *eikons* and lamps, and lined with illuminated pictures up to the very roof; and, finally, of pavement that goes up and down like a ploughed field, and *drojky*-drivers who insist on being paid thirty per cent. extra to-day, 'because it is the Empress's birthday.'

Literary scholars have argued, convincingly, that it was from Moscow, which Carroll depicts here in his journal as a fairground mirror-like city, with its vista offering reflection after reflection, endlessly warping back in on itself, that the author first had the idea for *Through the Looking-Glass, and What Alice Found There*, his 1871 sequel to *Alice's Adventures in Wonderland*.

On 5 August, Carroll and Liddon attended a special 6 a.m. service at the Petrovsky Monastery, on the anniversary of its consecration. Afterwards, they visited St Basil's Cathedral, which Carroll felt was 'as quaint (almost grotesque) within as without', and took a tour of the Treasury where they saw so many thrones, crowns and jewels that Carroll 'began to think that those three articles were rather more common than blackberries'. After dinner, they went to witness a Russian wedding in the cathedral, which Carroll deemed 'a most interesting ceremony', its highlight for him the recitations by a deacon with the most magnificent bass voice he'd ever heard.

The next day, and involving what it seems was a somewhat traumatic train journey, travelling 'by ordinary second class' as sleepers were 'unknown luxuries on this line,' they ventured to Nizhny Novgorod for the Makaryev Fair, Carroll declaring it a wonderful place. But 'all the novelties of the fair', he maintained, were 'thrown into the shade' by the

Tatar mosque and the sound of its call to prayer at sunset, which, he stated, 'floated through the air with an indescribably sad and ghostlike effect'.

But perhaps the pinnacle, spiritually, of the trip was to occur just over a week later. On 12 August, Bishop Leonide, Suffragan Bishop of Moscow, escorted them to the Troitsky Monastery and then presented them to Vasiliy Drosdov Philaret, the Metropolitan of Moscow and one of the most powerful and influential figures in the Russian Orthodox Church during the nineteenth century, in his palace.

Carroll and Liddon were to begin their journey homewards a week later, leaving Moscow for St Petersburg on 19 August, and wending their way back to Oxford via Warsaw (which Carroll believed was one of the nosiest and dirtiest towns he'd yet encountered), Wrocław (then Breslau), Giessen, Ems and Paris and Calais.

Carroll was never to leave England again and his Russian journal was not to be published until 1935, nearly forty years after his death. It was only then that devoted fans of Alice and her adventures were able to read of his encounters with real cities that were every bit as discombobulating as his brilliantly conjured-up wonderland.

▶ Matthew the Apostle on the roof of St Isaac's Cathedral, St Petersburg.

VENICE SIMPLON
ORIENT-EXPRESS
LONDON · PARIS · VENICE

Agatha Christie Boards the Orient Express

Trains are commonly to be encountered in the output of Agatha Christie (1890–1976). Their names, timetables and printed directories were pilfered by the prolific mystery writer for titles and plot devices in books such as *The Mystery of the Blue Train*, *The A.B.C. Murders* and *4.50 from Paddington*. The latter was re-named *What Mrs. McGillicuddy Saw!* for American readers, who it was feared might be less familiar with that particular London terminus. It was also while returning from a weekend at Christie's home in Devon that the publisher Allen Lane, finding nothing of interest to buy at the news kiosk on Exeter Station, hit on the idea of a range of cheaply priced, quality paperbacks. Among the opening ten titles of his new Penguin imprint was Christie's debut novel, *The Mysterious Affair at Styles*.

Originally published in 1921, this novel marked the arrival of one of detective fiction's most enduring and popular characters: the Belgian sleuth Hercule Poirot. An effete and physically diminutive moustache-waxer with astonishingly deductive 'liddle grey cells' and a frankly absurd accent, Poirot is a devilishly smart Continental, as only an English writer of the period could arguably conjure. But he was partly modelled after some Belgian refugees in Christie's native Torquay that she befriended while working at a local dispensary during the First World War, a job that was to equip her with an understanding of poisons. Knowledge that she later put to good use in her fictions when concocting fiendish means with which aggrieved wives might bump off their adulterous husbands or disgruntled factotums take revenge on their parsimonious bosses.

Similarly, Christie's personal familiarity with the routes, destinations, passenger types, porters, conductors, well-stocked dining cars and palatial sleeping carriages of a railway operated by La Compagnie Internationale des Wagons-Lits is what gives *Murder on the Orient Express* (re-titled *Murder in the Calais Coach* by her stateside publisher) its veracity. But her relationship to the Orient Express, a train that in the 1930s was a byword for exotic, intercontinental glamour, was far from that of an indolent tourist or passive commuter. Her initial journey on the train occurred during a period of emotional turmoil following the break-up of her first marriage to Archibald 'Archie' Christie. The train would, therefore, come to symbolize both her emancipation from the adulterous Archie and subsequently the birth and flourishing of a new partnership with her second husband, the archaeologist Max Mallowan, who was fourteen years her junior.

In its Belle Epoque prime, the Orient Express called daily at Vienna, ran twice a week to Budapest and thrice weekly to Istanbul (then Constantinople). The route was modified over the decades with the company going on to run various additional services, including one to Athens, and from 1919 a south-easterly sister train that ran via Lausanne, Milan, Venice, Belgrade and Sofia, known as the Simplon-Orient Express (after the Simplon Pass in Switzerland). And it was on this southern branch that Agatha Christie first ventured, second class, in 1928, and that Poirot journeyed fictionally in the novel six years later.

Christie's trip was precipitated by her agreement to a divorce from Archie. In her autobiography, published posthumously in 1977, she explains that with her marriage over and feeling the need to escape the gloom of an English winter she'd booked a holiday to the West Indies. But two days before she was due to depart, Christie went out to dinner with some friends in London and was introduced to a naval officer, Commander Howe, and his wife, who'd just returned from a posting in the Persian Gulf. They talked to her about Baghdad, a city that had entranced them, and urged the writer to visit it. Christie supposed 'one had to go by sea', but was delighted to be informed she could 'go by train – by the Orient Express'. As she wrote: 'All my life I had wanted to go on the Orient Express. When I had travelled to France or Spain or Italy, the Orient Express had often been standing at Calais, and I had longed to climb up into it. *Simplon-Orient Express – Milan, Belgrade, Stamboul ...*' The next morning she cancelled her tickets for the West Indies and exchanged them for a reservation on the Simplon-Orient Express to Istanbul with an extension from Istanbul to Damascus and from Damascus to Baghdad.

1 London
2 Istanbul (Constantinople)
3 Aleppo
4 Damascus
5 Baghdad
6 Tall al-Muqayyar (Ur)

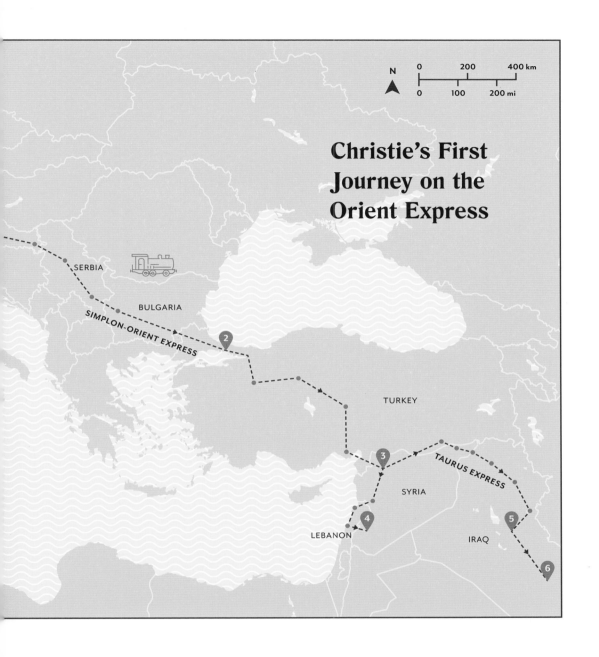

Christie's First Journey on the Orient Express

SERBIA

BULGARIA

SIMPLON-ORIENT EXPRESS

2

TURKEY

3

SYRIA

TAURUS EXPRESS

4

LEBANON

5

IRAQ

6

◀ **PREVIOUS PAGE** Vintage poster for the Venice Simplon-Orient Express.

As significant as her intended itinerary was the fact that she would be embarking on this voyage alone. For while she was a well-seasoned traveller, having undertaken a tour of the world in 1922, this was the first chance she'd ever had to indulge her passion for seeing places with no one to consider but herself.

The journey was, as she later recalled, 'all that I had hoped for'. After Trieste, Italy, and while passing through Yugoslavia and the Balkans, she remembered, 'there was all the fascination of looking out on an entirely different world: going through mountain gorges, watching ox-carts and picturesque wagons, studying groups of people on the station platforms, getting out occasionally at places like Nish and Belgrade and seeing the large engines changed and new monsters coming on with entirely different scripts and signs.' Solo travel suited her and she maintained that: 'Not until you travel alone do you realize how much the outside world will protect and befriend you.'

In Iraq, Christie visited the ancient Babylonian ruins at Ur (modern Tall al-Muqayyar) and struck up what would become a long-term friendship with the archaeologist Leonard Woolley and his wife, Katherine, who, as it turned out, had just finished reading one of the author's books, *The Murder of Roger Ackroyd*. When Christie returned to Ur the following year at their invitation, she was to meet Woolley's assistant Max Mallowan. Her stay was cut short when she received a telegram informing her that her daughter Rosalind was gravely ill with pneumonia. Fortunately Rosalind recovered but Mallowan escorted Christie back to London, the pair travelling part of the way home together on the Simplon-Orient Express. The same train heading west to east took them to Venice and Dubrovnik for their honeymoon later that same year.

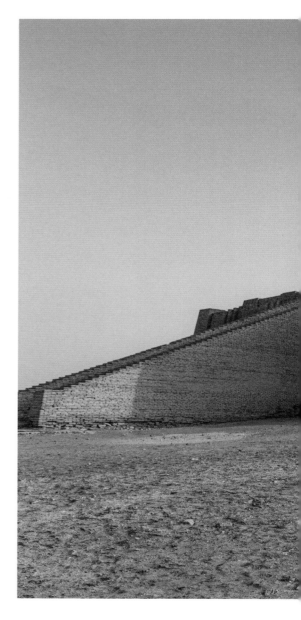

▶ Ruins of the Great Ziggurat of Ur, Iraq.

From now on, Christie was regularly to accompany Mallowan on his various archaeological digs across the Middle East and beyond to Egypt. These places, reached, more often than not, partially via the Orient Express, duly made their way into her novels: cue *Murder in Mesopotamia* and *Death on the Nile*. To avoid the region's excessive temperatures, Mallowan's excavations were almost always carried out in the winter months. And it is a noteworthy detail that this is the season in which *Murder on the Orient Express* is set; the train getting stuck in a snow-drift a vital component of its plot.

The novel opens with Poirot boarding a near-empty Taurus Express bound for 'Stamboul' at Aleppo at the ungodly hour of five in the morning and with quite a lot about the coldness of the weather and reports of snow in the Balkans. The Belgian declares high hopes of spending a few of days as a tourist in 'Stamboul' after his adventures in Syria. But not unlike Christie, he is immediately summoned back to London by an urgent telegram. As it is, he only just finds a berth on a surprisingly full for the time of year (and prevailing temperatures) sleeper carriage on the next Simplon-Orient Express for Calais.

We will draw a veil over what follows to prevent spoiling the story for anyone yet to read the novel or see either of its movie adaptations. But for those seeking a precise account of the interiors of the Wagons-Lits' midnight blue and gold-liveried rolling stock in this period, Christie, it should be said, is an indispensable resource. Likewise the litany

of times for departure and connections and the hours in which dining cars are open for breakfast, lunch and dinner supplied in the novel would have served a contemporary traveller almost as well as a Baedeker or *Bradshaw's Continental Railway Guide*. Poirot's fellow passengers too, an almost comically stereotypical international set (White Russian, Italian, English, Swede and American), are obviously a fairly representative sample of the kinds of people Christie herself encountered on her travels on the line. Though as far as we know, none of her real-life dining-car companions wound up dead from multiple stab wounds.

The Simplon-Orient Express itself might also be said to have suffered a slow lingering death of a thousand cuts, as it leached passengers after the Second World War and the eastern section of the route found itself behind the Iron Curtain in the emerging Cold War. The train was replaced by a slower and far more austere service with the almost Newspeak-ian title of the Direct Orient Express in 1962. This incarnation trundled gamely on for another fifteen years before being culled on 20 May 1977. But Christie, who died in the previous January, had long since forsaken it. Recalling another visit to Iraq in 1948, the year in which *Murder on the Orient Express* was published in paperback by Penguin for the first time, she wrote, again in her autobiography, 'No Orient Express this time, alas! It was no longer the cheapest way ... This time we flew – the beginning of that foul routine, travelling by air.'

◀ Istanbul.

Wilkie Collins and Charles Dickens Are Far from Idle in Cumbria

Aplaque with an unusually precise date adorns The Ship Hotel in Allonby, a small Cumbrian coastal resort on the Solway Firth. It records the stay of Wilkie Collins (1824–1889) and Charles Dickens (1812–1870) in this hotel on Wednesday, 9 September 1857. As the innkeeper's logbook shows, Collins and Dickens were, in fact, to put up here for the next two days, partaking of lunches with wine and beer and dinners with tea and brandy, along with taking lemonade and the dark beer porter during their spell here. The two writers had come north on a walking tour of the region just two days earlier, the pair disembarking at Carlisle on a train from Euston Station, London, on 7 September.

Collins, the son of a distinguished landscape artist, had been introduced to Dickens some six years earlier by the painter Augustus Egg. Twelve years younger than Dickens and then in the early stages of his career as a fiction writer, Collins was in awe of the older man. Recognizing Collins' nascent talent, Dickens was to take him under his wing, serving as a mentor and publishing the writer in his periodicals *Household Words* and *All the Year Round*.

Collins was to become, in the words of the biographer Claire Tomalin, 'Dickens' chosen companion for many of his escapes and jaunts'. And one possible motivation for this particular jaunt – other than its stated purpose to source colourful material for a series of travel pieces that was to be printed in *Household Words* under the title 'The Lazy Tour of Two Idle Apprentices' – was the cover it provided the unhappily married Dickens to see Ellen Ternan, an eighteen-year-old actress who Dickens had first met earlier that summer and who was then appearing in *The Pet of the Petticoats* at Theatre Royal, Doncaster.

When Dickens first proposed this excursion to Collins in a letter on 29 August, he wrote, conveying something of his conflicted emotional state, 'I want to escape from myself'. If initially claiming he didn't much care where they went, the end destination of their tour was never in any doubt, as Dickens had booked hotel accommodation for them in Doncaster before leaving London. The concluding article of their Lazy Tour detailed their impressions of this South Yorkshire city at its most boisterous during Race Week, when they maintained, 'a vague echoing roar of "t'harses" and "t'races" [was] always rising in the air, until midnight,' when it finally died away in 'occasional drunken songs and straggling yells'.

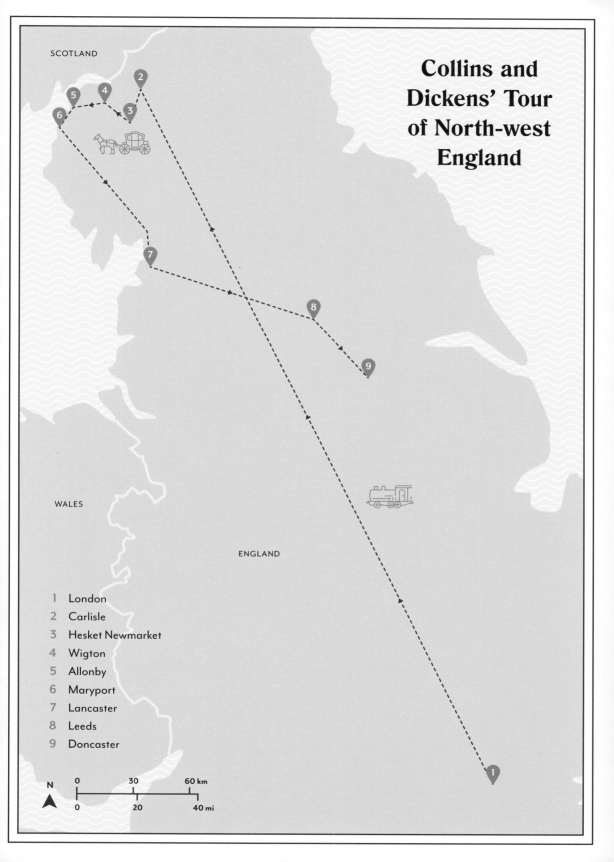

Collins and Dickens' Tour of North-west England

SCOTLAND

WALES

ENGLAND

1 London
2 Carlisle
3 Hesket Newmarket
4 Wigton
5 Allonby
6 Maryport
7 Lancaster
8 Leeds
9 Doncaster

N

| 0 | 30 | 60 km |
| 0 | 20 | 40 mi |

Their tour was to an extent bookended by animals. At its outset, Collins and Dickens had awoken after a night in Carlisle to find the city 'disagreeably and reproachfully busy' as it was market day and 'its cattle market, its sheep market, and its pig market' along with its corn market and street stalls and traders selling clogs, caps and the like were in full swing. Their response was to head off for the village of Hesket Newmarket, some 22 kilometres/14 miles away, where they checked into a cosy local inn and ate oatcakes and drank whisky, before going in search of 'a certain black old Cumbrian hill or mountain, called Carrock or Carrock Fell', which Dickens was anxious for them to climb. Collins less so. His hesitancy was perhaps well founded. On the afternoon of their ascent it was raining heavily and the mountain was soon enveloped by 'a canopy of mist much thicker than a London fog'. Their compass got broken and they lost their way, and Collins managed to sprain his ankle as they blindly groped down the mountainside into the valley below. After a change of clothes and dosing themselves with more whisky (imbibed by Dickens, applied with oil to Collins' injury to help relieve the pain and bring the swelling down), they went on to the market town of Wigton in a little covered carriage. Here Collins was ferried to the home of a Dr Speddie for more conventional medical treatment.

From Wigton they journeyed on to the watering-place of Allonby, where it was possibly hoped that the briny air and views of the coast of Scotland might help restore Collins' spirits. The village, whose chief claim as a resort was the presence of a donkey on its sands, was pleasant enough but possessed only limited diversions. Leaving a still-prone Collins on The Ship Hotel's sofa, Dickens had to walk out to nearby Maryport to collect his mail. The pair eventually decided to venture on to Lancaster, from where they made, briefly, for Leeds and then, at last, Doncaster.

THE RAILWAY STATION AT DONCASTER.

After its first run in *Household Words* between 3 and 31 October 1857, 'The Lazy Tour of Two Idle Apprentices' was never reprinted in Dickens' lifetime. But the writers' northern adventure (or really misadventure in Collins' case) would leave a deeper mark in the annals of literature. When Collins came to write *The Woman in White* two years later, he set parts of the novel in areas of Cumbria they'd passed through. Ewanrigg Hall, just outside Maryport, served as the basis for Limmeridge House in that book, which, incidentally, was first serialized in Dickens' journal *All the Year Round*.

◀ The summit of Carrock Fell in the Lake District, England.

▲ *The Railway Station at Doncaster, The Illustrated London News*, 15 September 1849.

▶ Portrait of the actress Ellen Ternan, c.1860.

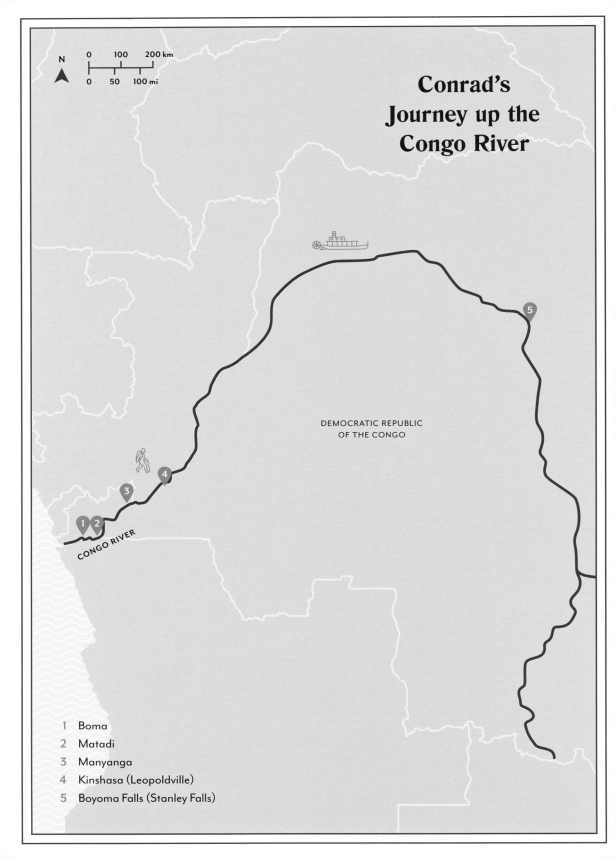

Conrad's Journey up the Congo River

DEMOCRATIC REPUBLIC
OF THE CONGO

CONGO RIVER

N

0	100	200 km
0	50	100 mi

1 Boma
2 Matadi
3 Manyanga
4 Kinshasa (Leopoldville)
5 Boyoma Falls (Stanley Falls)

Joseph Conrad Sees True Horror in the Congo

In reference to his own experiences in the Belgian Congo and their basis for his 1899 novel *Heart of Darkness*, Joseph Conrad (1857–1924) once stated that it was 'pushed a little (and only a very little) beyond the facts of the case'. Born Józef Teodor Konrad Korzeniowski in Podolia, a province of the Polish Ukraine, the author, who as a small boy had relished the popular nautical adventure novels of Captain Frederick Marryat, went to sea aged just sixteen, and his career as a sailor carried him around the globe.

West Africa was one place that Conrad had always vowed to visit, ever since imbibing stories about the expeditions of European explorers like Mungo Park, whose doomed attempt to follow the Niger to its source was the stuff of *Boy's Own* legend. The opportunity finally presented itself to the author in 1891, when he was offered the command of a Belgian steamer in the Congo Free State after its previous captain, the Dane Johannes Freiesleben, had been murdered after a quarrel with some local men. If a slightly ominous set of circumstances in which to step into a job, it actually wasn't the first time Conrad had assumed a post vacated by the violent death of a predecessor. Eager to work and keen to see Africa, he signed up for a full three-year term with the Société Anonyme Belge pour le Commerce du Haut-Congo, the major trading company operating in the Congo basin. He was to last only six months, and what he underwent there scarred him for life, mentally and physically.

From 1865 to 1908, the Congo Free State was owned in its entirety by the Belgian King Leopold II. Conrad, like many white Europeans, had swallowed the official Belgian line that they were saving the country from barbarism. Such self-serving propaganda, used to justify the colonial occupation, subjugation and wholesale exploitation of African people and the plunder of the continent's resources would not stand up to close scrutiny, as Conrad was soon to discover for himself.

The author's journey to Africa began in Bordeaux, where on the 10 May 1891 he left this French port aboard the *Ville de Maceio*, which called in first at Tenerife in the Canary Islands before continuing south along the western coast of Africa. The vessel stopped off in Dakar in Senegal, Conakry in Guinea, Freetown in Sierra Leone, Cotonou in Benin and Libreville in Gabon, before arriving at the mouth of the Congo River and sailing on to Boma, the capital of the Congo Free State, which it reached on 12 June 1891.

The following day, Conrad took a steamer upriver to Matadi, where he was to be billeted with Roger Casement, the Irish republican campaigner, diplomat and British consul officer knighted for his forensic exposés of the abuses of indigenous peoples in Congo and Peru, later executed for treason. Casement was almost the only other European in Africa of whom Conrad wholeheartedly approved. Recording their first encounter in his diary on 13 June, he wrote: 'Made the acquaintance of Mr. Roger Casement, which I should consider as a great pleasure under any circumstances and now it becomes a positive piece of luck. Thinks, speaks well, most intelligent and very sympathetic.'

The pair were to spend the next two weeks in each other's company before Conrad and another company man, Prosper Harou, left with a caravan of twenty-one men on 28 June to join his ship in Kinshasa (then Leopoldville). However, since the

stretch of the Congo River between Matadi and Kinshasa was unnavigable, and a railway line linking them was still under construction, this journey had to made on foot. The trek proved arduous, with dead bodies left to putrefy under the blistering sun littering their path and mosquitoes a constant menace. Conrad and Harou, who'd succumbed to a fever and had to be carried much of the way, got to Kinshasa, exhausted and ailing, on 2 August.

Assigned now to the *Roi de Belges* steamer, which had a crew of thirty Africans, Conrad ventured upriver to Boyoma Falls (then Stanley Falls), observing as he went the appalling petty cruelties of Belgian ivory hunters and company functionaries, the chain gangs of Congolese toiling in conditions of utter squalor, scores of villages abandoned or left

▲ Matadi, Democratic Republic of the Congo.

in ruin and swathes of countryside picked clean by felling. The *Roi de Belges* docked at Boyoma Falls on 1 September and six days later set off downstream to Kinshasa. Among the passengers now taken on board was Georges-Antoine Klein, a commercial agent with the Société Belge stationed in Boyoma Falls. Klein was gravely ill with dysentery and would not survive this return voyage. He is one of a number of potential candidates it has been suggested as a possible model for the monstrous ivory trader Kurtz in *Heart of Darkness*, who also dies of a jungle fever while being ferried downriver on a steamer.

By the time the *Roi de Belges* reached Kinshasa on 24 September, Conrad had himself come down with malaria and dysentery. He would suffer bouts of ill health for the rest of his remaining few months in the Congo, sickness only adding to his sense of despondency and disillusionment. After completing his final steamer run on 4 December, he resigned and sailed back to Europe from Boma a couple of weeks before Christmas. Pitching up in London on 1 February 1891, and looking by all accounts half dead with fever, Conrad would spend nearly a decade brooding on what he'd seen in the Congo before converting it into fiction. *Heart of Darkness*, when it first appeared, was to be one of the most damning indictments of colonialism ever written.

▼ *Boma, on the Congo River, The Graphic*, volume XXVIII, no. 712, 21 July 1883.

▶ NEXT PAGE Congo River, Democratic Republic of the Congo.

Isak Dinesen in and out of Africa

I sak Dinesen is the male pseudonym under which the Danish author Karen Blixen (1885–1962) generally published. Such is the writer's current status in her native Denmark, that a portrait of her graces the nation's 50-kroner banknote. But her homeland, to begin with, reacted rather coolly to her first serious literary efforts. Her debut book, *Seven Gothic Tales*, a collection of stories of the uncanny influenced by *One Thousand and One Nights* and the work of Robert Louis Stevenson, was written in English and became a surprise bestseller in America after being rejected by almost every publisher going. Blixen's own relationship to Denmark was complicated by her love for Africa and specifically Kenya, which she regarded as an Eden from which she'd been banished after being forced to return to the family seat in Rungsted, just north of Copenhagen, in 1931.

She'd left Denmark some eighteen years earlier, a headstrong twenty-eight-year-old on the brink of marriage and full of hope for her new life as the wife of Baron Bror von Blixen-Finecke, an aristocratic Swedish farmer in British East Africa. She came back a financially ruined divorcee. Her marriage and the farm, which she'd run herself since 1921, had failed ignominiously. Her health was compromised by the syphilis acquired from her adulterous former husband and only a few months earlier her lover,

Denys Finch Hatton, a blue-blooded British big-game hunter, had been killed after crashing his Gypsy Moth aeroplane while out on safari. Writing was to be her path to recovery, and *Out of Africa*, her 1937 memoir and most famous work, would serve 'in part as a sublime repair job', as her biographer Judith Thurman astutely phrases it, for the calamity of much of her life in Africa.

The die for this tragedy arguably was cast from the moment Von Blixen-Finecke abandoned plans to run a dairy farm in Kenya and opted instead to invest their money in the Swedo-African Coffee Company and acquired 1,821 hectares/4,500 acres for a coffee plantation upland from Nairobi at the foot of the Ngong Hills. Unbeknown to him, the soil was too acidic and the rains too erratic to grow coffee profitably there, and the venture was pretty much doomed from the start. Once the deal on the plantation had been signed, Blixen was to follow Bror to Kenya, and marry him on her arrival in Mombasa.

Blixen's family set aside their (many) misgivings about Bror's business sense and his suitability as husband material and came to Copenhagen to see her off in early December 1913. She first travelled south with her mother and father to Naples, where they stayed for two weeks, before boarding the *Admiral* on 16 December. The journey to East Africa was to

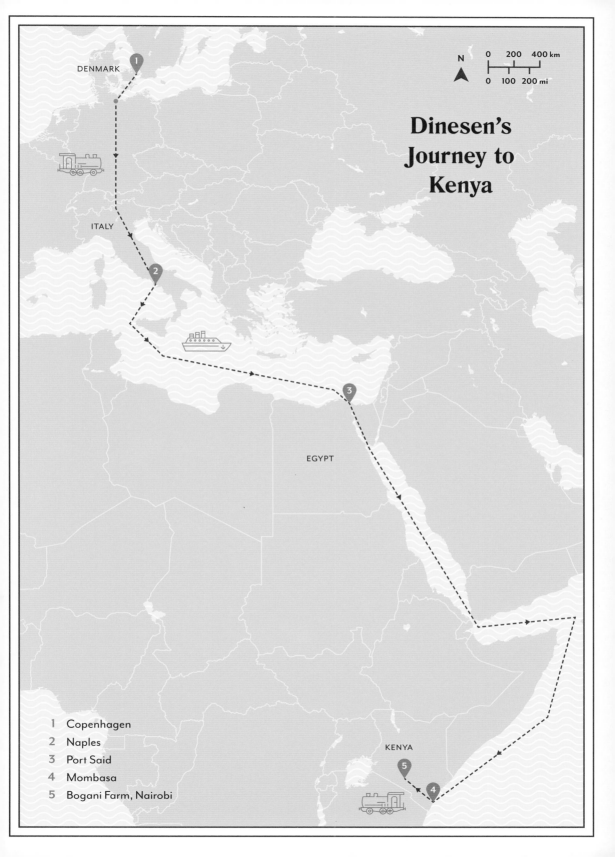

Dinesen's Journey to Kenya

DENMARK

ITALY

EGYPT

KENYA

N

| 0 | 200 | 400 km |
| 0 | 100 | 200 mi |

1 Copenhagen
2 Naples
3 Port Said
4 Mombasa
5 Bogani Farm, Nairobi

take nineteen days, the ship steaming through the Mediterranean and the Suez Canal into the Red Sea and the Gulf of Aden to the Indian Ocean, after which it followed the Somali coast south to Mombasa.

The *Admiral* reached Kilindini Harbour on 13 January 1914, and Bror came aboard to claim his bride. After a night at the Mombasa Club, their wedding took place the following morning with Prince Wilhelm of Sweden acting as one the Baron's witnesses. At 4 p.m. the wedding party escorted the newlyweds to the railway station, where they were ushered into a private dining carriage (put at their disposal by the Governor of the Protectorate) on a train for Nairobi. The train, running on the Uganda Railway trunk line route from Mombasa to Lake Victoria, didn't have any sleeping carriages so the Blixens were to spend their wedding night bunked up on a banquette.

From Nairobi it was a further 19 kilometres/12 miles to the farm, where all 1,200 of its field hands had gathered to greet their new mistress. Their uproarious welcome annoyed Bror but utterly enthralled Blixen. Her affinity for this place and its native peoples

was instantaneous. In her twilight years she once remarked of the Africans that, 'They came into my life as a kind of answer to some call in my own nature'. Alienated by the British colonists whose exploitation of native labour she thoroughly disapproved of, Blixen was to claim, at the start of the First World War and when rumours were spread that she was a German spy, that she felt less foreign among the Somalis and native Kenyans, who were more 'like brothers' to her than the local English residents.

Her former home in Kenya, a grand bungalow, which she called 'Bogani' or 'Mbogani' (literally 'house in the woods'), is now a national museum dedicated to her life and work and relationship with the country. It first opened in 1986, shortly after a Hollywood movie adaptation of *Out of Africa* starring Meryl Streep as Blixen was released, bringing the author a whole new generation of readers.

◀ Karen Blixen on safari in Kenya, c.1918.

▼ Blixen's former home, now a museum, at the foot of the Ngong Hills, Kenya.

Sir Arthur Conan Doyle Discovers the Perfect Place to Bury Sherlock Holmes

Has there ever been a writer quite so contemptuous of his most famous and most loved literary creation than Sir Arthur Conan Doyle (1859–1930) was of Sherlock Holmes? The consulting detective, along with his sidekick chronicler Dr John H. Watson, first appeared in *A Study in Scarlet* in *Beeton's Christmas Annual* in 1887. This novella-length story was written in between Doyle's examinations of nautical malingerers and Senior Service retirees at his medical practice in Southsea, Hampshire.

Holmes was not an instant hit. But once more stories featuring the character (subsequently published as *The Adventures of Sherlock Holmes*) began to be serialized in *The Strand* magazine in 1891, the fictional occupant of 221B Baker Street became a sensation. While Holmes lifted Doyle forever out of financial penury, its author chafed against him, believing that the aesthete sleuth was preventing him from getting on with better things. His disenchantment with his golden goose set in early; scarcely had Holmes' first run in *The Strand* ended than Doyle wrote to his mother announcing his intention to kill off the character. She replied, 'You won't! You can't! You mustn't!' He didn't, postponing the death for a further two years.

As he later explained in his autobiography, 'the difficulty of the Holmes work was that every story

really needed as clear-cut and original a plot as a longish book would do'. And he could not 'without effort spin plots at such a rate' as the reading public and his publishers now seemed to demand.

After producing two series of Holmes, Doyle believed that he was in danger of being entirely identified with what the writer dismissively regarded as 'a lower stratum of literary achievement'. As a sign of his resolution he determined to end the life of his hero. If his motive was clear, the means and the method were only to present themselves to him while on a tour of Switzerland.

In August 1893, Doyle was invited to Lucerne in Switzerland to give a lecture, and chose to extend this visit into a vacation with his wife Louise (affectionately known as 'Touie'). While boarding at the Hotel de L'Europe, Doyle made the acquaintance of the Methodist minister and author Silas Hocking, who was surprised to find the creator of Sherlock Holmes such a beefily robust and hale and hearty fellow. Tall and strong, with a snub nose, slightly piggy eyes and a great moustache that was waxed at the ends, Doyle was closer physically (and temperamentally and professionally as a former medical man) to Watson than the thin, hawk-nosed Holmes. Something that many have commented on then and since. To his further annoyance, the author was often addressed as Mr Sherlock Holmes.

Doyle's Vacation in Switzerland

SWITZERLAND

1 Lucerne
2 Meiringen
3 Reichenbach Falls
4 Zermatt
5 Findel Glacier

N

0   5   10 km
0   3   6 mi

Perhaps it was little wonder then that Doyle would be moved to further comment that at this time he 'had such an overdose of [Holmes]' that he felt toward him as he did 'toward pâté de foie gras' which he once ate too much of, its name giving him 'a sickly feeling' ever after.

From Lucerne, Doyle and Touie travelled to Meiringen, 25 kilometres/15 miles east of Interlaken. A fictionalized version of their journey, albeit one larded with an additional layer of ominous foreboding, would eventually be given to Holmes and Watson in 'The Adventure of the Final Problem', the good doctor relating that:

For a charming week we wandered up the Valley of the Rhone, and then, branching off at Leuk, we made our way over the Gemmi Pass, still deep in snow, and so, by way of Interlaken, to Meiringen. It was a lovely trip, the dainty green of the spring below, the virgin white of the winter above; but it was clear to me that never for one instant did Holmes forget the shadow which lay across him. In the homely Alpine villages or in the lonely mountain passes, I could tell by his quick glancing eyes and his sharp scrutiny of every face that passed us, that he was well convinced that, walk where we would, we could not walk ourselves clear of the danger which was dogging our footsteps.

At Meiringen, the Doyles headed to the nearby Reichenbach Falls, a fearsome cascade that was already listed as one of the sights of the northern Swiss alps in guidebooks for English travellers.

After Meiringen and the Reichenbach Falls, the couple moved on to Zermatt. Booking into the Riffelalp Hotel, Doyle was pleased to discover Hocking was staying there too. The pair, along

◀ PREVIOUS PAGE Lake Lucerne, Switzerland.

◀ Sidney Paget's illustration showing Sherlock Holmes and Professor Moriarty about to fall to their deaths at Reichenbach Falls, Switzerland.

with a priest called Benson, and aided by a local guide, were to undertake an expedition to the Findel Glacier, east of Zermatt. In his memoirs, and written some years after the fact, Hocking was to recall that while they were strolling on the glacier and 'making detours to avoid crevasses' Doyle raised the matter of disposing of Holmes. The author supposedly told them, 'I intend to make an end of him. If I don't he'll make an end of me'. Benson, a fan, was horrified by the idea and tried his best to persuade Doyle against it. But Hocking was curious to learn how he intended to finish him off. When the author confessed he still wasn't sure, Hocking claimed he proffered the suggestion that having him fall to his death down just such an icy crevasse as the ones they were gingerly avoiding wouldn't be a bad way to go. Doyle, apparently, agreed with a chuckle.

But back home in England later that summer, when the author came to pronounce Holmes' last rites, it was Reichenbach Falls that spoke to him most. It was, as he put it in his autobiography, 'a terrible place and one I thought would make a worthy tomb for poor Sherlock, even if I buried my banking account along with him'. In the final (and famous) reckoning between Holmes and his nemesis, the master criminal Professor Moriarty, they were to disappear over the edge of the precipice, still clutching each other mid-struggle, their bodies seemingly dashed on rocks below and/or claimed by the icy torrents of the falls. An accompanying illustration by Sidney Paget, showing the two men tussling at the top of the cascade in the last seconds before their doom would practically be seared into the collective consciousness of late Victorian society.

Even though news of Holmes' death had been leaked a month before the story's publication in December 1893, 'The Adventure of the Final Problem' was greeted with stunned disbelief by the public. Black mourning armbands were said to have been worn for Holmes. Letters were sent to the author and petitions raised calling on Doyle to resurrect him. Perhaps as many as 20,000 people cancelled their subscriptions to *The Strand* magazine in protest. All to no immediate avail, Doyle expressing only indifference to their cries. Relieved to be rid of Holmes, the writer promptly embarked on a new series of historical tales set in the Napoleonic period and featuring a French Hussar named Brigadier Étienne Gerard.

Those, however, still yearning for Holmes would have to wait until 1901, when Doyle eventually relented and revived the character in *The Hound of the Baskervilles*. Unfortunately for Doyle (but fortunately for lovers of detective fiction), its enormous success shackled the writer to the character afterwards for close to thirty more years.

▶ The Matterhorn, the Swiss Alps.

F. Scott Fitzgerald Bathes in the Light on the French Riviera

F. Scott Fitzgerald's (1896–1940) literary brilliance as the witty and worldly wise chronicler of the Jazz Age and his youthful, suntanned good looks were regularly commented on during his heyday in the 1920s. Later, in the light of what followed, they were recalled in sorrow, anger and disappointment. By the time the writer died in Hollywood in 1940, this once-golden boy was a severely tarnished alcoholic, all but forgotten by the reading public; *Tender Is the Night*, the novel he'd slaved over for nearly ten years, was a critical and commercial failure and out of print, and original unsold copies of *The Great Gatsby* were still going begging.

Still, in the epoch when Fitzgerald first blazed on to the literary scene, a suntan remained a daringly modern thing: a badge of leisured cosmopolitan sophistication for those who could afford it. Its newfound vogue in the aftermath of the First World War – and its subsequent promotion, with the aid of Coco Chanel in the pages of *Vogue* – owed a good deal to the near-simultaneous adoption of the French Riviera as summer destination by a set of sun-worshipping artistic Americans, including Fitzgerald, his wife, Zelda, and Gerald and Sara Murphy.

Fitzgerald dedicated *Tender Is the Night* to the Murphys (the book's tribute runs, 'To Gerald and Sara—Many Fêtes'), and the couple were the inspiration for Dick and Nicole Diver, the novel's glamorous protagonists. Though Dick, a psychiatrist who loses it to drink over the course of the novel,

notoriously morphs into a version of the author himself, while the beautiful, neurotic Nicole was based far more closely on Fitzgerald's mentally unstable wife than the real-life Sara.

Sara was the eldest daughter of a millionaire Cincinnati ink manufacturer, and partially raised in Europe, where she mingled in German and British aristocratic circles. Gerald was the Yale-educated second son of a well-read owner of a prosperous New York luxury goods store. Subjected to family opprobrium about their marriage (Sara's father was particularly unhappy about her choice of husband) and repelled by the stuffiness of materialist, elite American society, the Murphys had moved to Paris in 1921. Another motivating factor in their transatlantic migration was that exchange rates were immensely in their favour. The imbalance between the US dollar and the French franc allowed them to live well on a smaller share of Sara's trust fund, thereby avoiding further awkward questions about Gerald's career prospects and his semi-abandoned study of landscape architecture at Harvard into the bargain. A similar financial calculation was also to bring the more cash-strapped Fitzgeralds to France. Something that the writer would describe in 'How to Live on Practically Nothing a Year' – a humorous piece for *The Saturday Evening Post* in 1924 on the advantages of slumming it on the Continent.

In the early summer of 1922 – a literary *annus mirabilis* in which James Joyce's Ulysses and T.S.

Eliot's *The Waste Land* were published, and the temporal setting for *The Great Gatsby* – the Murphys headed to Houlgate, a seaside resort in Normandy that was then popular with fashionable Parisians. While there, though, they were invited to join the composer Cole Porter (a friend of Gerald's from Yale) and his wife, Linda, in a villa they'd rented in Antibes in the south of France. Gerald would later credit Porter with always having 'a great flair, a sense of the avant garde, about places' and when speaking to the *New Yorker* magazine in 1962, reiterated that at that time 'no one ever went near the Riviera in summer'. Porter never returned to Antibes. But the Murphys were smitten.

The following year they persuaded the manager of the Hôtel du Cap at Antibes to keep his establishment (which usually closed on 1 May) open with a skeleton staff for the summer and a return visit. A precedent was established. And the pioneering Murphys, having encouraged friends and other like-minded, free-spirited types to join them, now worried about losing their unspoiled idyll to incomers. They responded by purchasing a house at 112, chemin des Mougins on the slope of Golfe-Juan in Antibes, where they would entertain in high, if informal style. They christened the property Villa America, and had it remodelled on modern art deco lines with a Moroccan-style flat roof, expressly for sunbathing.

These renovations were, however, still ongoing when the Murphys returned to Antibes for the summer of 1924 and so they booked themselves once more in to the Hôtel du Cap. It was here that the Fitzgeralds visited them that August, the couples

1	Hyères
2	Saint-Raphaël
3	Antibes
4	Juan-les-Pins
5	Cap d'Antibes

FRANCE

N

| 0 | 5 | 10 km |
| 0 | 3 | 6 mi |

◀ PREVIOUS PAGE Antibes, France.

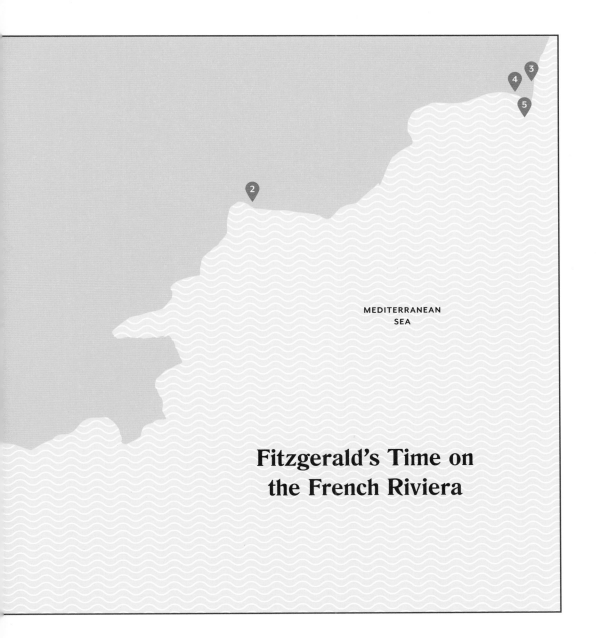

MEDITERRANEAN
SEA

Fitzgerald's Time on the French Riviera

having met in Paris that spring. Fitzgerald was to open *Tender Is the Night* with a description of the Hôtel du Cap, which he fictionalized as Gausse's Hôtel des Étrangers, and perhaps even more fruitlessly (since its true identity was obvious to everyone), sought to disguise it ever so slightly by pinking-up its white walls:

> On the pleasant shore of the French Riviera
> ... about half way between Marseilles and the
> Italian border, stands a large, proud, rose-
> colored hotel. Deferential palms cool its flushed
> façade, and before it stretches a short dazzling
> beach ... The hotel and its bright tan prayer rug
> of a beach were one.

Like the youthful Rosemary Hoyt and her mother at the start of the novel, the Fitzgeralds had journeyed to the Riviera from Paris by train. Initially lodging in the sleepy coastal town of Hyères, which Zelda considered dreary, they soon moved to Saint-Raphaël, which Fitzgerald characterized as 'a little red town built close to the sea, with gay red-roofed houses and an air of repressed carnival about it'. It was in a rented house here, Villa Marie, that Fitzgerald knuckled down to work on *The Great Gatsby* – the blinking green beam of the lighthouse off shore at Cap d'Antibes has been held as the probable inspiration for light on the dock that signals Jay Gatsby's yearning for Daisy in the novel.

Zelda, meanwhile, left with little to do, embarked on a brief, if possibly unconsummated, love affair with Edouard Jozan, a dashingly handsome and darkly tanned young French aviator. On discovering his wife's infidelity, Fitzgerald fell into a jealous rage and kept Zelda locked in her room until she promised never to see Jozan again. Their marriage, if already turbulent, would start to go from bad to worse; and

◀ Front cover of the first edition of *Tender Is the Night*, 1934.

▲ F. Scott Fitzgerald, Scottie and Zelda at Antibes, France, 1926.

Zelda's mental health with it. She nevertheless was to remember Jozan in her semi-autographical novel *Save Me the Waltz*, giving the book's heroine, Alabama Beggs, an extramarital romance in the French Riviera with a pilot named Jacques Chèvre-Feuille.

The Fitzgeralds were to spend most of the next five summers in the Riviera, including two years running at Villa St Louis, a house on the sea wall in Juan-les-Pins, where the writer, having finally completed *The Great Gatsby*, appears to have been as his most content. 'With our being back in a nice villa on my beloved Riviera (between Nice and Cannes)', he reported in one letter, 'I'm happier than I've been for years. It's one of those strange, precious and all too transitory moments when everything in one's life seems to be going well.'

Inevitably, it was not to last. The Wall Street Crash, the premature death of the Murphys' beloved son Patrick in 1929, Fitzgerald's uncontrolled drinking and Zelda's increasing instability were all to call time on those glorious summers in the south of France. Fitzgerald's attempts to convey them in book form, a process seriously hindered by his alcoholic intake, would win him few admirers when *Tender Is the Night* was published in 1934. At the height of the Great Depression, the novel was savaged by critics as a decadent throw-back and the book appalled the Murphys; Sara, especially, was hurt and angered by it. Yet it stands as a curious, if flawed, picture of a time and a place, an odd kind of testament to the Riviera's importance to Fitzgerald, and the effect, both good and ill, it had on his life and writing.

▶ The French Riviera.

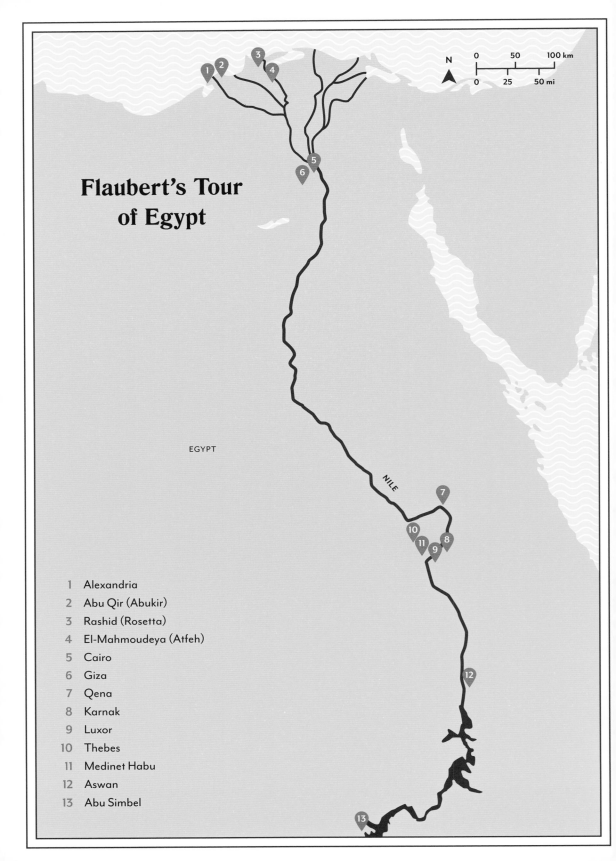

Flaubert's Tour
of Egypt

EGYPT

NILE

1 Alexandria
2 Abu Qir (Abukir)
3 Rashid (Rosetta)
4 El-Mahmoudeya (Atfeh)
5 Cairo
6 Giza
7 Qena
8 Karnak
9 Luxor
10 Thebes
11 Medinet Habu
12 Aswan
13 Abu Simbel

Gustave Flaubert Indulges Himself in the Orient

On 14 September 1833, a ship carrying a massive piece of stonework entered the Harcourt quay in Rouen, France, a port city on the Seine around 128 kilometres/80 miles north-west of Paris. The *Louxor* had sailed from Egypt nearly two years earlier with the obelisk of Ramses II on board. This 25-metre/82-foot-tall pink granite edifice had spent the previous 3,000 years or more standing guard outside Ramses II's temple, beside the Nile at Luxor. But it was now destined for its new home at the Place de La Concorde in Paris. Among those who gathered on the quayside to gaze in wonder as this chunk of the ancient world floated into view in Normandy was an eleven-year-old Gustave Flaubert (1821–1880). The youngest son of a distinguished surgeon, Flaubert's penchant for all things Eastern had been formed even earlier by nursery-room readings of the *Arabian Nights*, and would grow stronger still once he entered adolescence and feasted on the works of Lord Byron and Victor Hugo.

An inveterate scribbler from almost the moment he could hold a pen, writing plays for the family at nine, Flaubert was a compulsive daydreamer who aged just fifteen became romantically fixated on Elisa Schlésinger, a married woman some eleven years older than him. As the late, great Flaubertian scholar Francis Steegmuller was to note, the one true love of Flaubert's life, the free-spirited poet and author Louise Colet, would also be a married woman eleven years his senior.

Flaubert himself was never to marry, and when young made frequent use of prostitutes. In a letter to Colet he candidly admitted, 'It may be a perverted taste, but I love prostitution, and for itself, too, quite apart from its carnal aspects. My heart begins to pound every time I see one of those women in low-cut dresses walking under the lamplight in the rain.' And when the author of *Sentimental Education* did eventually get to tour what was then broadly termed 'the Orient' in 1849, he was to take full advantage of the services of sex workers wherever he went.

While Flaubert's older brother, Achille, had willingly entered the medical profession, an outcome that surprised no one, as both their father and their mother's father had been doctors, the would-be writer showed no aptitude or desire to follow in his brother, father or grandfather's footsteps. He continued to pin his hopes on literary fame. At eighteen, presented with the choice of studying either medicine or law, he opted for law. The one significant outcome of this decision was that he struck up a firm friendship with Maxime Du Camp, one his fellow students in Paris.

But Flaubert's legal education was to come to an abrupt end when over the Christmas and New Year vacation of 1844–5 he suffered a complete collapse and was diagnosed with epilepsy. (Though the precise nature of his illness and that diagnosis have always been disputed.) His ailments were considered serious enough to allow him to withdraw from his studies. Back in Rouen, after a brief sojourn to Italy in

▼ Cairo.

the belief that the country's more temperate climate might help improve his health, Flaubert holed up in his study to toil for sixteen months on an epic novel, *The Temptation of St Anthony*.

In the meantime, Du Camp, a wealthy orphan, had not only ventured to North Africa and Turkey but also published an acclaimed account of his travels. For his next adventure, Flaubert's friend had a more ambitious journey in mind; one that he dearly hoped to undertake with his former college friend and that would see the two men explore Egypt and return by way of Syria, Palestine, Cyprus, Crete and Rhodes. Flaubert's mother, if initially resistant to such a lengthy excursion and arguing that her son's condition might just as easily be enhanced by a spell in Madeira, finally gave her blessing to the trip.

Preceding their departure, nevertheless, was to be an excruciating episode where Flaubert subjected Du Camp and his other close friend, Louis Bouilhet, to a four-day-long reading of his newly completed novel. After which, both men urged Flaubert to burn all 451 pages of his overblown manuscript and move on to something else. Ideally, they recommended, to the author's horror, he should write something set in the present day and more in the realist ilk of Honoré de Balzac. Despite bristling at these suggestions at the time, Flaubert, would take them on board when he consequently came to write *Madame Bovary*.

Du Camp, ever the more practically minded of the pair, was not only to draw up the itinerary for their voyage but also obtained official commissions for them both. Flaubert, unlikely as it might seem (and indeed proved), was expected to gather information on Egyptian sea, river and caravan trade and farming for the French Ministry of Agriculture and Commerce. Meanwhile, Du Camp's role was to take photographs of Egyptian antiquities for the Ministry of Public Instruction. The latter's job required them to travel with a hulking pile of still-primitive photographic equipment. The visitors' mission was considered important enough that they were to be provided with armed bodyguards for parts of their tour to prevent locals interfering (or making off) with their gear. During their travels, Du Camp was to produce the sole photograph of Flaubert in his youthful prime; the writer snapped in the garden of their hotel in Cairo, wearing the native costume of a red tarboosh (a cap resembling a fez) and flowing white cotton robe. One of this hotel's proprietors was a certain Monsieur Bouvaret, an ex-actor whose surname it has been suggested possibly provided Flaubert with the monikers for both Emma Bovary and François Bouvard, who appears in his final unfinished novel, Bouvard and Pécuchet.

Progressing south via Djion, Chalon and Lyon, by stagecoach, steamboat and train, they reached Marseilles on All Saints Day (1 November) 1849, and from there they sailed on Le Nil, a three-masted packet ship with a steam-driven paddle and a single funnel, to Malta. The crossing to North Africa was so bad, however, that the ship was forced to turn back. And it wasn't until 15 November, after a further five days at sea, that Le Nil was able to approach the Egyptian port of Alexandria. Flaubert, despite his weak constitution, had weathered the choppy ocean journey better than Du Camp and his Corsican valet Sassetti (both of whom suffered with appalling seasickness), and had enjoyed strutting about the deck with a cigar in his mouth during the swells and imagining himself to be a Byronic voyager out of Childe Harold's Pilgrimage.

Flaubert would decry Alexandria as 'almost a European city', commenting in letters home and his journal on the numbers of Western visitors and a surfeit of smart hats. Nevertheless, he was entranced by his initial glimpse of the dome of Muhammad Ali's seraglio; charmed beyond belief that the first thing he clapped eyes on upon drawing up to Alexandria's

shore was a driver with a pair of camels; and overwhelmed by the cacophony of noise and 'bellyful of colours' that greeted them when they landed.

Lodged in the Hotel d'Orient, and armed with official letters of introduction, Flaubert and Du Camp paid visits to the French-born Egyptian military commander Soliman Pasha and Harim Bey, the Minister of Foreign Affairs, took in the sights, witnessed a parade to celebrate the circumcision of the son of a rich merchant and, naturally, went to a brothel. Du Camp, according to Flaubert, was impatient to sample what might be on offer, be that women or boys. In this particular establishment, in a street behind their hotel, the courtesans were female and a litter of kittens had to be removed from the divan before the author could engage in congress. The pair were to avail themselves of far lower, bed-bug-ridden houses over the coming months, indulging their appetites and seemingly insatiable libidos without the slightest fear of censure this far from home.

Before leaving for Cairo, the Frenchmen undertook a ride 64 kilometres/40 miles along the Mediterranean coast to Rashid (then Rosetta), where the famous hieroglyphic stone had been found, stopping to lunch en route at the fort at Abu Qir (Abukir). After sailing on the Nile and being shown a tree that was worshipped as minor deity, they rode back to Alexandria and on 25 November boarded a crowded steamer for El-Mahmoudeya (then Atfeh), where they would change on to a larger overnight ferry to Cairo.

Du Camp's diligence in photographing virtually every monument they encountered and the degree to which, prostitutes aside, this work dominated their itinerary would begin to grate on Flaubert. The thrill of seeing the Pyramids and Sphinx at Giza, which left him giddy with excitement, gradually faded to be replaced with 'monument-boredom', in Steegmuller's winning phrase. But this torpor was to evaporate at

Thebes, where the author's enthusiasm for relics of Ancient Egypt was renewed in spades. Writing to his mother in May 1850, and in sorrow at finally having to leave the tombs, temples and ruined halls of Luxor, Karnak and Medinet Habu behind as they headed on to Qena and the Red Sea, he described Thebes as 'a place where one could stay ... in a perpetual state of astonishment'. At Luxor too, he saw Rameses II's remaining obelisk – the identical twin of the one that had passed through Rouen all those years earlier. Thinking of its sibling in Paris, he mused sentimentally on how much it must miss the Nile and be bored by the Place de la Concorde and its taxis, when chariots would once have roared by its feet in days gone by.

Two months later, Flaubert and Du Camp would conclude their time in Egypt, sailing from Alexandria for Beirut and beginning nearly a further year of travel through Syria, Turkey, Greece and Italy. Du Camp would later urge Flaubert to publish an account of their travels, as he himself did. But while, as Steegmuller notes, 'passages in the Carthaginian novel, *Salammbô*, the Palestinian tale, *Herodias*, and the final version of his *Temptation of Saint Anthony* ... bear a close relationship' to 'portions ... of notes he made in Egypt' he never did. His experiences there were to rid him of his naively adolescent purple prose, his travel notes hardening his observational powers. And when he returned to his home in Croisset, on the outskirts of Rouen, he would – having seen the 'real Orient' for himself – leave aside stories of high-flown exoticism in distant times and places and begin work on a new novel. That book, *Madame Bovary*, would land him in the dock but ensure his place in the literary canon.

▼ The Sphinx and Pyramids, Giza, Egypt. Photograph by Maxime Du Camp, c.1850.

Johann Wolfgang von Goethe Gets Lost in Italy

On 28 August 1786, Johann Wolfgang von Goethe (1749–1832) celebrated his thirty-seventh birthday in the Bohemian town of Karlovy Vary (then Karlsbad). For the previous decade the poet, playwright, scientist and author of *The Sorrows of Young Werther* – the novel that catapulted him to literary fame at twenty-four – had served as the Privy Counsellor to the Duke and Duchess of Weimar. Enjoying the close confidence and respect of the young duke and his wife, Goethe's roving ministerial brief saw him variously responsible for the finances of the duchy, its mines and even for a time, its war department. But the onerousness of his duties and the stuffiness of court life had gradually driven the poet to the brink of a nervous breakdown. After most of the courtiers had returned to Weimar a few days after his birthday, Goethe begged the duke for a leave of absence and then made the hastiest of departures imaginable. At 3 a.m. on 3 September, he simply jumped into a public coach and left without a servant (almost unthinkable for a man of his class and position) and with hardly any luggage.

As he was to explain in a letter to the duke, the task of assembling an eight-volume collection of his works to date for publication, several of which remained unfinished or in need of heavy revisions, had been weighing heavily on his mind:

I have undertaken it all rather lightly, and I am now beginning to see what is to be done if it is not to become a mess. All this and much else impels me to lose myself in places where I am totally unknown. I am going to travel, quite alone, under another name, and I have great hope for this venture, odd as it seems.

He adopted the pseudonym Jean-Philippe Möller for his clandestine adventure. However, his true identity was rumbled only a day into his travels when he was recognized by a star-struck assistant in a bookshop in Regensburg. Goethe, according to his diary, opted to front the situation out. Looking the assistant squarely in face, he calmly denied it was him and beat a speedy exit from the shop.

Shortly before accepting the position at Weimar back in 1775, Goethe's father had urged his son to visit Italy, which he had toured as a young man. And it was south and to Rome that the poet was ultimately bound. His dream was to live the life of a modest artist (for a while anyway), rather than that of a famous writer or esteemed, if put-upon, statesman. And his artistic endeavours were to result in one of the most notorious incidents of these travels. Having paused to sketch a ruined fortress at Malcesine, on the border between Austrian- and

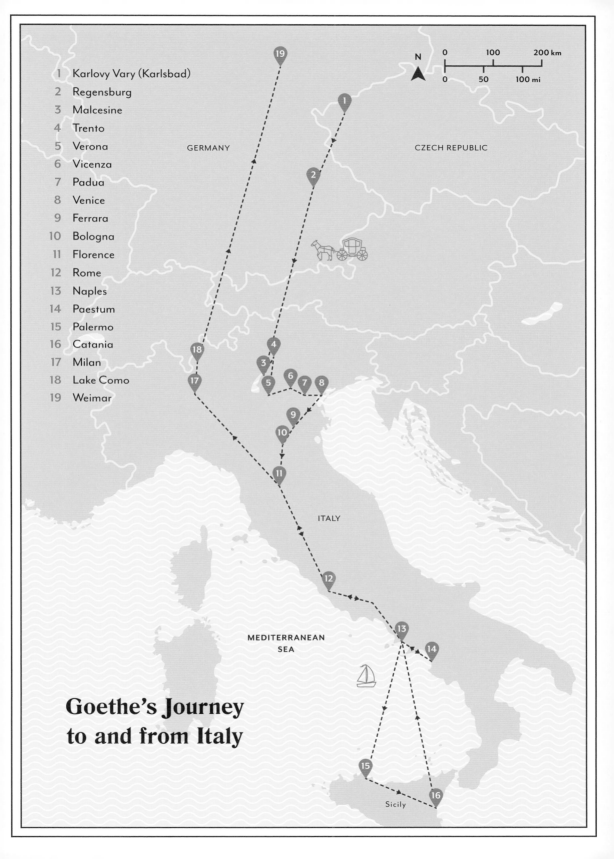

1 Karlovy Vary (Karlsbad)
2 Regensburg
3 Malcesine
4 Trento
5 Verona
6 Vicenza
7 Padua
8 Venice
9 Ferrara
10 Bologna
11 Florence
12 Rome
13 Naples
14 Paestum
15 Palermo
16 Catania
17 Milan
18 Lake Como
19 Weimar

GERMANY

CZECH REPUBLIC

ITALY

MEDITERRANEAN
SEA

Sicily

**Goethe's Journey
to and from Italy**

Venetian-held territories, Goethe was nearly arrested as a spy. His subsequent progress through Trento, Verona, Vicenza and Padua was observed discreetly, if with some interest, by the Venetian authorities.

The writer had aimed to travel as inconspicuously as possible. To that end Goethe went so far as to don elements of Italian costume, sporting the kind of 'linen netherstocks' worn by the Vicenzan market-goers, and deliberately adopted the mannerisms he observed in Verona in order to blend in. Voyaging in this unorthodox way and disguised in local garb, he succeeded in preserving his anonymity all the way to Venice. Delighted at being able to move about freely without fear of being recognized for the first time in years, he relished passing for a merchant and especially enjoyed milling about unknown in the Venetian crowds. Seeking to lose himself, quite literally, Goethe took to ambling about Venice without a map and scoping out its remotest quarters. Drinking

in its carnivalesque atmosphere, his head was often left spinning by the combination of the city's theatrical sights and the appalling stench from its canals.

From Venice, Goethe went to Ferrara, Bologna and Florence, spending a mere three hours in the latter in his haste to reach Rome. Arriving in Rome on 29 October, he sought out J.H.W. Tischbein, a German artist in residence there, whose paintings he'd championed and with whom he'd struck up a fitful correspondence. The painter secured Goethe lodgings in the Corso, and the writer was to spend the next four months in the city. In the opinion of his biographer John R. Williams, it was 'in retrospect at least – to be one of the happiest and most fulfilling times of his whole life'. The German was fascinated by Rome. If dismissing its

◀ *Portrait of Goethe in the Countryside*, J.H.W. Tischbein.

▲ Ponte Pietra, Verona, Italy.

carnival as noisome and lacking 'genuine gaiety', he busied himself with sightseeing, sketching and reading and even did a spot of writing. The city appears to have restored his *joie de vivre* and galvanized his creative energies. Hearing, however, that the dormant volcano Vesuvius had become active again, Goethe left Rome for Naples on 22 February 1787. On this occasion travelling in the company of Tischbein, who would join Goethe in one of the three ascents he made of the smouldering Vesuvius and on an excursion to the ruins of Pompeii. The volcano dutifully laid on a suitably impressive eruption for the Germans, while Pompeii charmed by being smaller and more compact than expected; Goethe compared it to a mountain village buried in snow.

In Naples, Goethe was to abandon anonymity and sought the company of the city's more illustrious citizens. Among them the English ambassador Sir William Hamilton and his future wife (and more famously Admiral Nelson's future mistress), Emma Lyon, who Tischbein painted posing in classical dress.

Goethe and Tischbein parted company in Naples, the writer sailing on to Sicily on 29 March 1787 with Christoph Heinrich Kneip, another young German artist. Recommended by Tischbein as a potential travelling companion, Kneip had already accompanied Goethe on a visit earlier that month to the ruined Ancient Greek city of Paestum near Salerno as something of a trial run. The passage to Palermo would prove difficult, their tiny corvette alternately buffered and becalmed by unfavourable winds. Fending off seasickness by holing up in his cabin, Goethe still found the strength and inspiration to begin revising the first two acts of his play *Torquato Tasso*.

▼ *Johann Wolfgang von Goethe Visiting the Coliseum in Rome*, Jakob Philipp Hackert, c.1790.

▶ Mount Etna, Sicily, Italy.

▼ Lake Como, Italy.

Sicily was to offer further sites of archaeological, geological and culinary interest. Goethe was particularly taken with the quality of Sicilian lettuces, which he maintained tasted of milk. He and Kneip were to inspect lava flows that had almost destroyed Catania in 1669 and poked about the crater rim of the still lively Monte Rosso, having been warned off attempting to scale the rather more volatile Mount Etna itself. On Sicily too, Goethe would manage to meet the humble relations of Alessandro Cagliostro. One of his age's most notorious swindlers, Cagliostro's immoral antics and capacity for duplicity would be mined by the writer for the demon Mephistopheles in *Faust*.

Goethe's hopes that the crossing back to Naples in mid-May would be quicker this time and that he might recover from seasickness sooner were to be dashed. Their ship came close to being wrecked on the rocks off Capri, and no amount of bread and red wine could steady his sea legs. After a few weeks in Naples, Goethe headed back to Rome. Here, after obtaining an extension to his leave of absence from the Duke of Weimar, he was to largely settle for the next ten months. He was finally to leave the city for his homeland on 23 April 1788, but did not reach Weimar until 18 June 1788, after choosing to make a stop off in Florence and wending back via Milan and Lake Como.

Goethe had gone to Italy to get lost. But his trip provides an exemplary (almost clichéd) example of someone who, in effect, found both himself and a renewed sense of purpose by travelling. Thirty years were to elapse before Goethe published *Italian Journey*, his account of this sabbatical. But his impressions of the country and studious engagement with its Renaissance and Greco-Roman heritage were to colour almost everything he did afterwards. Not least the acceptance that his talents lay with words on the page and for the stage. Painting and drawing, if continued with a passion throughout his life, were never to be indulged with quite the same precedence again.

Graham Greene Learns to Love Life Again in Liberia

In the summer of 1934, Graham Greene (1904–1991) was struggling to provide for his young family with the meagre income from his writing. After hitting a critical and commercial streak with his fourth novel *Stamboul Train*, Greene was now so sick of fiction that he claimed he'd 'rather get the bubonic plague than write another novel for a year'. Yet he needed to write to earn a living and decided that as travel books were then popular he would pen one himself. Greene had, as he later confessed, never been out of Europe and not very often been outside England. But hoping to appeal to the Anglo-American reading public's taste for accounts of relatively obscure and out of the way places, he chose to go to Liberia.

When later called upon to explain why he chose this West African republic, a politically troubled country founded in 1822 with a bequest from American philanthropists as a home for freed slaves, he stated bluntly that, 'like Everest, it was there'. One key factor was that Greene most likely had a commission from the Anti-slavery Society. (He would present a lecture to the society on conditions in the country shortly after returning from Liberia.) But no less important in the eventual decision to go there was persuading his younger cousin Barbara Greene to accompany him on the adventure. A vivacious

twenty-three-year-old debutante, more naturally at home in London's Chelsea salons and West End nightclubs, Barbara claimed she'd never even been on a camping trip before this.

The Greenes' African odyssey began on 4 January 1935, when the pair took the 6.05 p.m. train from London's Euston Station to Liverpool. After spending the night in the Adelphi Hotel, they joined five other passengers on the *David Livingstone*, a cargo ship heading to Freetown, the capital of Sierra Leone, via the Bay of Biscay, Madeira, Las Palmas in Gran Canaria and Banjul (then Bathurst) in the Gambia. Greene and Barbara, much to the writer's annoyance, were snapped by a photographer from the *News Chronicle* as they stepped on to the gangplank. The paper subsequently reporting their departure under the sensationalist (and racist) headline 'BEAUTY OF 23 SETS OUT FOR CANNIBAL LAND.'

In *Journey Without Maps*, Greene's published account of their trip, he was to assert that in some pockets of Liberia, especially the north-eastern region occupied by the Mano people, cannibalism had not died out entirely. But this claim is widely refuted by contemporary anthropologists. The title of Greene's book was, nevertheless, largely a statement of fact, since he and Barbara were to venture into parts of the interior of Liberia; territories of thick bush that could only be reached on foot and that certainly few urban residents of the Liberian capital of Monrovia concerned themselves with.

Greene and Barbara were only to spend a short time in Freetown before heading up country to the border of Liberia. They were to travel 290 kilometres/180 miles by train for two whole days on a narrow-gauge railway to Pendembu, then take a truck to Kailahun on the edge of Guinea and from there trek 32 kilometres/20 miles to an American mission at Bolahun just inside Liberia itself. They were to reach the mission on 16 January.

Before leaving Freetown, however, they hired two local boys, Amedoo and Laminah, to act as guides-cum-servants and Souri, an elderly cook. Over the course of their journey, they would go on to recruit as many as twenty-five carriers at a time to help them lug the vast quantity of luggage they'd packed. Their baggage, according to Barbara, included 'beds, tables, chairs, several big wooden cases of food, a water filter, the money box, two suitcases and all kinds of odds and ends'.

Their eventual route was to take them along the north of the county through Pandemai, Duogobmai in Lofa Country (the latter a place Greene maintained was 'so horrible there was nothing else to do but drink') and Zigida – of which the novelist would state, 'even in the light of morning it was evil'. They then ventured south through Galaye and Dieke with the aim of getting to Buchanan (then Grand Bassa) and sailing along the shore to Monrovia. Along the way they photographed religious ceremonies; despaired of the heat, dust, ants, rats and snakes; marvelled at the honesty and steadfastness of their hired help; and had encounters with friendly villagers, loathsome colonial officers, dubious indigenous traders and corrupt officials.

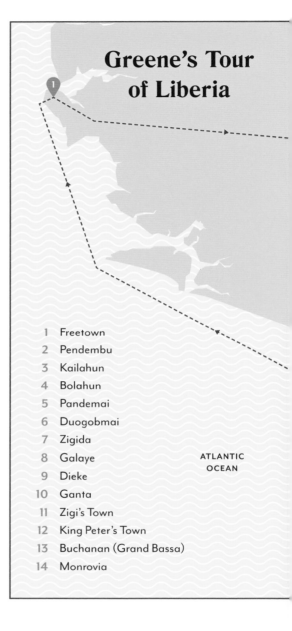

Greene's Tour of Liberia

1 Freetown
2 Pendembu
3 Kailahun
4 Bolahun
5 Pandemai
6 Duogobmai
7 Zigida
8 Galaye
9 Dieke
10 Ganta
11 Zigi's Town
12 King Peter's Town
13 Buchanan (Grand Bassa)
14 Monrovia

ATLANTIC OCEAN

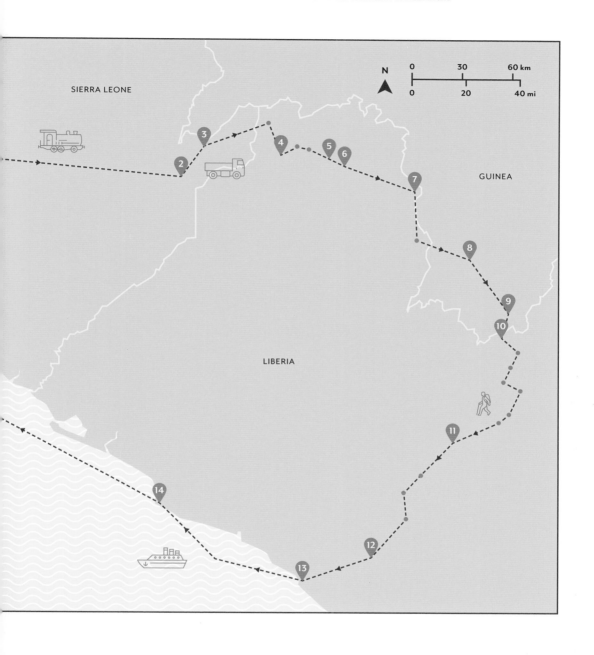

SIERRA LEONE

GUINEA

LIBERIA

N

| 0 | 30 | 60 km |
| 0 | 20 | 40 mi |

◀ PREVIOUS PAGE Freetown, Sierra Leone.

While Barbara was generally ferried about in a hammock, Greene usually walked to save on the additional expense. By his own estimation, he seldom covered less than 24 kilometres/15 miles a day, and in the final stage of their journey between Ganta and the sea the novelist came down with a fever and eventually had to submit to being carried. At Zigi's Town, still a good seven days' walk from Buchanan, Barbara became gravely concerned for her cousin's health, and, knowing of his Catholicism, was terrified that he might die without receiving the appropriate rites. Fortunately, Greene rallied the next morning. The Greenes also received news that day that they might be able to get a lorry to meet them at Harlingsville and drive them the last leg. And their spirits were further lifted when outside King Peter's Town they came upon a Seventh Day Adventist mission and were treated to iced fruit drinks and gingerbread by the German missionary's wife, who struck Barbara as the picture of a middle-class hausfrau.

At Buchanan, they managed to squeeze themselves on to a boat bound for Monrovia that was overladen with 150 opposition politicians. These men were going to the capital to stage demonstrations against the upcoming presidential elections, which were likely to be rigged, and they all became

uproariously drunk on fermented cane juice over the course of the seven-and-a-half-hour sea voyage.

The Greenes stayed in Monrovia for just nine days. They were by now anxious to return home and caught the *MacGregor Laird* on 12 March. Four days later the ship docked at Freetown and soon after left for its ultimate destination, Dover. Green and Barbara landed in the Kentish port in early April. Here, the cousins separated; Barbara immediately returning to London and Greene meeting his wife in one of the town's hotels.

As his official biographer Norman Sherry was to observe, Greene's excursion to Liberia was to be 'the first of his exploratory journeys' and established a relationship with Africa that would see him stationed in Freetown in 1942 to undertake war-time intelligence work; an experience that would inform his novel *The Heart of the Matter* published six years later. For the travel writer Tim Butcher, who retraced Greene's momentous journey, the 'trip changed forever [Greene's] attitude to mortality and risk' for it was in Liberia and lying 'near death, flitting in and out of consciousness in the worst moments of his sickness' that the writer, as he himself later put it, 'learned to love life again'.

◀ Red dirt road through the bush near Kailahun, Liberia.

▼ Paperback cover of *Too Late to Turn Back*, Barbara Greene's memoir of her travels in Liberia with her cousin Graham Greene.

Hermann Hesse Goes East in Search of Enlightenment

It was nearly two decades after winning the Nobel Prize for Literature in 1946 and just a few years after his death that Hermann Hesse (1877–1962) suddenly became quite the hip literary name to drop among the tuned-in, turned-on children of the flower power generation. Dr Timothy Leary, the sacked Harvard psychologist and chief proselytizer for psychedelic drugs, went so far as to advise, 'Before your LSD session, read *Siddhartha* and *Steppenwolf*'. It is unlikely Hesse would have welcomed this development, disliking collective movements of all sorts, and adolescent enthusiasts of his works especially. But his books, often featuring dogma-defying protagonists seeking lone paths to self-fulfilment and spiritual enlightenment beyond Western traditions, struck a particular chord with younger readers in the 1960s and 1970s.

In 1911, Hesse, with his marriage in trouble and only months after the birth of his third son, Martin, left Europe to embark on a hastily arranged odyssey to the East. Accompanied by his friend, the painter Hans Sturzenegger, the author, after two days' travel through Germany, Switzerland and Italy, boarded the *Prinz Eitel Friedrich* in Genoa on 6 September. Hesse was supposed to be heading to India; a country where both his parents and his grandparents had worked as missionaries.

His interest in all things Eastern had been largely stirred by the colourful stories he'd heard from his maternal grandfather, Hermann Gundert, a man who inspired admiration, fear and reverence when he was growing up. A talented linguist who spoke more than thirty languages and compiled Malayalam–English dictionaries and grammars, Gundert spent twenty-three years in southern India, most of them in Thalassery (then Tellicherry) in Kerala studying the local languages and dialects and spreading the word of (his Christian) God.

Hesse never reached his final intended destination, his excursions only extending as far east as Indonesia, Malaysia and Sri Lanka (Ceylon). For while Hesse certainly inherited many qualities from his grandfather, a tolerance of more tropical climes, it was soon to become clear, was not something he shared with his formidable ancestor. The *Prinz Eitel Friedrich* had barely cleared Naples before the author started to find the heat oppressive. The food, largely British to cater for colonial tastes, also disagreed with him, and he suffered with diarrhoea and couldn't sleep without dosing himself with pills. The other passengers, with their languid, apathetic expressions and self-important European assumptions, didn't meet with his approval either; they seemed to represent everything he was supposedly trying to escape.

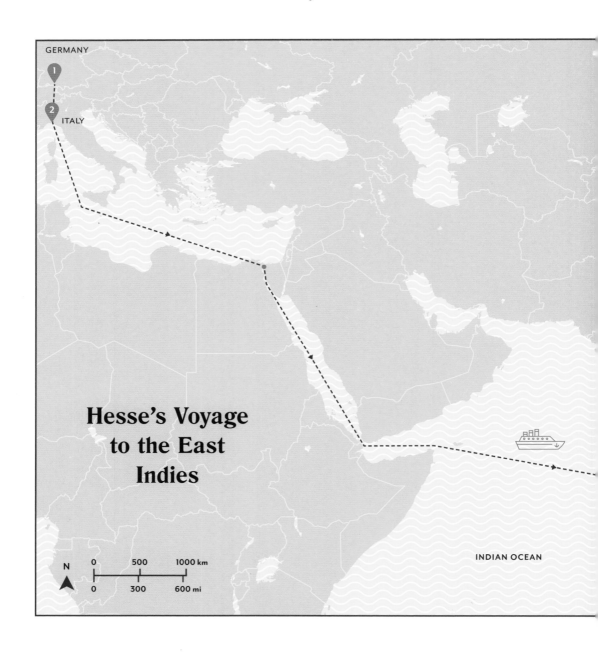

GERMANY

1

2 ITALY

Hesse's Voyage
to the East
Indies

INDIAN OCEAN

N

| 0 | 500 | 1000 km |
| 0 | 300 | 600 mi |

◀ PREVIOUS PAGE Elephants
in Sri Lanka.

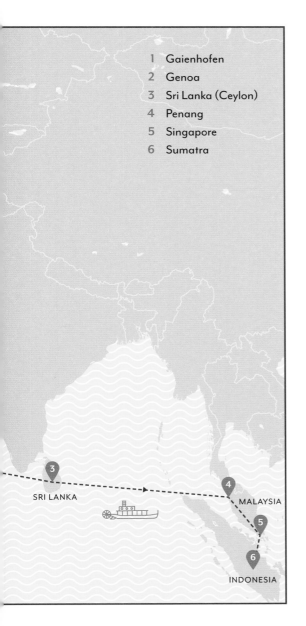

1 Gaienhofen
2 Genoa
3 Sri Lanka (Ceylon)
4 Penang
5 Singapore
6 Sumatra

SRI LANKA

MALAYSIA

INDONESIA

A few years later, Hesse would write more romantically about their first Eastern stopover, Penang in Malaysia, recalling how the surging life of this Asiatic city burst upon them, the Indian Ocean 'glittering between innumerable coral islands', and how they stared in 'astonishment at the many coloured spectacle of street life' there, a 'wild, colourful human swarm in the ever crowded alleys' and a 'sea of candles at night'. But in truth at the time the author was more repelled than enchanted, hating the smells, dirt, poverty and the incessant beggars and street traders. And if admiring the Chinese, he recoiled from the Malayans, who he deemed overexcitable and also somehow too obsequious to their colonial oppressors. From Penang, Hesse and Sturzenegger sailed to Singapore, where the writer would tour the city in a rickshaw. From there, the two friends crossed the equator on a Dutch steamer that deposited them in southern Sumatra.

Hesse's disenchantment was to grow stronger still. A journey on a small Chinese riverboat to Palembang brought Hesse nearly to the end of his tether. The humidity of the jungle, whose green liana vines he feared could seize him, and the insects, along with the dysentery he had contracted, drove him to distraction.

Hesse and Sturzenegger happily left Sumatra for Sri Lanka, which by comparison to Sumatra, he judged a 'paradise island with its fern trees and palm-lined shores', but the climate and conditions proved really no more agreeable to the writer. At Kandy, the capital of the country's central province, Hesse, by now subsisting on red wine and opium, was nearly too ill to undertake his intended pilgrimage to Dalada Maligawa, the sacred Buddhist shrine whose great temple houses what is said to be one of the Buddha's teeth. But having managed that, he seems to have rallied enough to then scale Ceylon's highest point, the mountain

▶ The German ship *Prinz Eitel Friedrich*, which carried Hesse from Italy to the East Indies, interned at Newport, Virginia, USA, March 1915.

at Pidurutalagala. The ascent seems to have invigorated Hesse's spirits, if also clarifying his need to leave Asia as soon as was possible. He and Sturzenegger hauled themselves on to the *Maras*, a Chinese steamer sailing for Singapore, and once there caught practically the first boat heading back to Europe. India was never to be reached. Nevertheless and somewhat confusingly, Hesse would title an account of his travels, in which he wrote largely negatively about what he'd seen of Asia, *Reports from India*.

If what he'd seen of the continent was a disappointment, his engagement with the sacred books of the East – the Vedas, Upanishads, Bhagavadgita and the Theravada Buddhist Suttas – was only to intensify upon his return. *Siddhartha*, written between 1919 and 1922 and during a period when Hesse also encountered Alfred Hillebrandt's *From the Brahmanas and Upanishads*, was to be the product of that reading. The novel, which is set in India in the fifth century BC, relates the story of Siddhartha, the son of a Brahmin priest, who must leave his faith and family to discover the truth for himself. The India it depicts is mythic. And perhaps, therefore, all the more universal for not being based on a place that might have shone less brightly had Hesse actually visited it for himself.

▲ *Self-portrait in Studio Coat*, Hans Sturzenegger.

▶ Sunset over the Straits of Malacca, Penang, Malaysia.

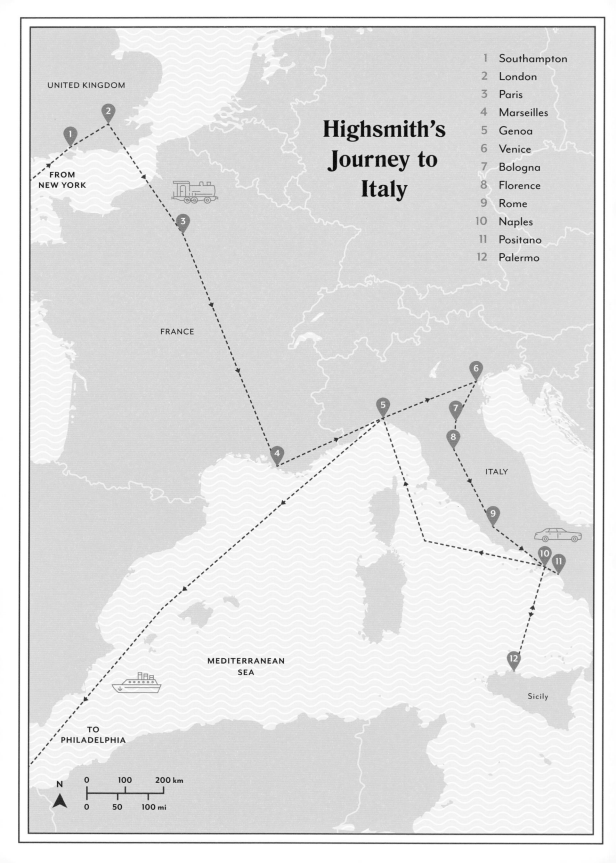

Patricia Highsmith Spots a Likely Character in Positano

One of modern fiction's most compelling creations, surely, is Patricia Highsmith's (1921–1995) Thomas Ripley. The suave, sexually ambiguous, shape-shifting, amoral thief, fraudster and murderer, who appears in a series of five of her novels, made his debut in *The Talented Mr Ripley* in 1955. In that opening book, Ripley was dispatched to Italy, first class all the way and with a $1,000 meal ticket, to retrieve Richard 'Dickie' Greenleaf, the errant son of a wealthy American industrialist. What follows, though, is a novel that raises questions about our capacity for evil, the difference between appearances and reality and the construction of personal identities. Highsmith herself identified closely with her chameleon-like psychopathic protagonist, even signing letters 'Pat H, alias Ripley'. The character was inspired by a real person that the writer encountered while visiting the Italian village of Positano on the Amalfi Coast for the second time in 1952.

A native of Texas in the United States, Highsmith had made her first visit to Italy – and Europe – in 1949, shortly after learning that *Strangers on a Train*, her debut novel, had been accepted for publication. She paid for the trip with savings accrued from writing for comic books for ready cash and money cadged from her family. If predominately, though not exclusively, attracted to women, at the time of her departure from New York on 4 June, Highsmith had just become engaged to the English writer Marc Brandel. Over the course of her voyage across the Atlantic to Southampton, England, on board the *Queen Mary*, and while bashing out stories in frustration at travelling in tourist class and having to share a cabin with four other women, she was to decide that the marriage would be untenable and resolved, initially unsuccessfully, to end the relation.

A further impetus for Highsmith abandoning any serious thoughts of future conventional wedded bliss, though, was to be provided on the Continent by a female lover. On the first leg of her trip, Highsmith stayed in London with her soon-to-be British publisher Dennis Cohen and his wife, Kathryn, an intelligent, attractive former actress. Kathryn was to show Highsmith the sights and escorted her on an excursion to the theatre at Stratford-upon-Avon in Warwickshire. The writer was quickly smitten by the older, more sophisticated woman. But Highsmith's itinerary meant that she soon had to leave England for the European mainland.

A boat train from London's Victoria Station led her first to Paris, which the author adored for both its squalor and splendour. From there she went south to Marseilles and on to the Italian cities of Genoa, Venice, Bologna, Florence and Rome. Feeling sick and lonely in Rome, she wrote to Kathryn imploring her to come out to Italy and join her; the pair eventually arranging to meet in Naples, Highsmith's next intended destination.

The city of Naples, with its crumbling ruins and ragged, insanitary streets teeming with noisy life, instantly thrilled Highsmith. Each day brought a cacophony of church bells, barking dogs and car horns lasting from dawn to dusk. Kathryn was to arrive in Naples on 3 September, and four days later the two women and another friend were to take a drive to Positano. The idyllic fishing village on the Amalfi Coast, situated in what the writer would describe as 'an ideal rock-bordered cove' was to occupy a unique place in her life and her creative output. Kathryn and Highsmith were to become lovers shortly after this initial outing there, their fleeting affair kindled on a boat back from Sicily, their next port of call, and continued in Naples in the few weeks before Highsmith sailed from Genoa to Philadelphia on 23 September.

Highsmith was to be back, though, just three years later, with her new partner Ellen Hill, an emotionally unstable and domineering sociologist who nagged Highsmith about her drinking and domestic slovenliness. The pair, whose relationship was, according to her biographer Andrew Wilson, 'a tortured one from the beginning', had travelled to Positano from Florence at the beginning of June 1952, and as part of an extended two-year-long peripatetic tour of Europe. There they were to check into the Hotel Albergo Miramare, which boasted fine views of the Gulf of Salerno and the Mediterranean Sea. One morning during their stay at this cosy establishment, at around 6 a.m., Highsmith wandered out on to the balcony of their room and spied a figure walking alone on the sands of the beach below. As she later was to recall, 'All was cool and quiet, the cliffs rose high behind me ... then I noticed a solitary young

man in shorts and sandals with a towel flung over his shoulder ... There was an air of pensiveness about him, maybe unease.' Although Highsmith never saw the man again or ever learned his name, she was captivated by his image and two years later would use it as the foundation for Thomas Ripley.

Positano was to receive its due in *The Talented Mr Ripley* too. Renamed Mongibello, the village is where Ripley inveigles his way into the lives of Dickie Greenleaf and his girlfriend Marge, the couple treating a house there as a base-cum-coastal-retreat and a tranquil spot to do the kind of serious idling known only to those born to money. Sadly, Positano is less tranquil than it was in Highsmith's day. When the film director Anthony Minghella came to make his version of *The Talented Mr Ripley* in the late 1990s, he deemed the whole region of the Amalfi Coast unsuitable as it was too scarred by development. He, therefore, opted instead to shoot the Mongibello scenes on the islands of Ischia and Procida.

▶ Naples.

▶ NEXT PAGE: Positano, Italy.

Jamaica and Haiti Cast a Spell on Zora Neale Hurston

Zora Neale Hurston (1891–1960) was part of the Harlem Renaissance, a flourishing of African-American writers, poets, playwrights, artists and musicians in New York shortly after the First World War, dedicated to producing work that gave voice to the Black experience and engaging with their African heritage, free of white stereotypes and prejudices. She first began to make her mark on that scene in the 1920s in the theatre, collaborating with the likes of the poet Langston Hughes. In the next decade, though, she was to find much wider international fame as both an acclaimed novelist and a pioneering folklorist.

A protégé of the German-American anthropologist Franz Boas at Barnard College, Hurston would conduct some of her earliest anthropological fieldwork in Harlem itself. But in 1927, and with encouragement from Boas, she returned to her native Florida to undertake a survey of Black folklore in the American south. This research would furnish her with the material for her first non-fiction book, *Mules and Men*. It was published in 1935, just a year after *Jonah's Gourd Vine*, her debut and semi-autobiographical novel; much of which was also set, naturally enough, in Florida and her hometown, the all-Black municipality of Eatonville.

On 16 March 1936, the writer received the news that she'd been awarded a grant of $2,000 from the Guggenheim Foundation for a 'study of the magical practices among Negroes in the West Indies'. This long-cherished project was to take her away from the United States for close to sixteen months, seeing her spend nearly a year in Jamaica and Haiti, and returning to the latter country to complete her immersion in the island's voodoo customs for a further four months from May to September in 1937.

Before her departure, however, she needed to settle a personal matter. Hurston, a thrice-married divorcee in her middle forties, had been engaged in a passionate relationship with Percy Punter, a graduate student at Columbia some twenty years her junior. She later described it as 'the real love affair of my life'. Punter wanted Hurston to marry him, give up her career and set up home with him outside New York. Unable to contemplate the loss of her hard-fought personal and professional independence, Hurston used the trip as the justification to call time on their romance.

She sailed for the Caribbean from New York, landing in Haiti on 13 April 1936. After a day-long pit-stop in the Haitian capital, Port-au-Prince, where she introduced herself to the appropriate authorities in preparation for her return in six months' time, she boarded a boat to Jamaica, then still a British colony. Hurston was to be taken aback by some of the interracial frictions between Jamaica's various Afro-Caribbean communities and the poor lot afforded to Black women on the island. One man she spoke to in the mountainous coastal parish of St Mary maintained that women who pursued careers 'were just so much wasted material'.

Nevertheless, Hurston, as a visiting American with academic credentials, was generally afforded more respect than her Jamaican sisters and given an accolade never previously bestowed on any woman, when, again in the parish of St Mary, a goat was slaughtered for a celebration to be held in her honour – this ritualistic feast of heavily spiced goat was traditionally staged under moonlight and always a major event in the parish. Hurston was similarly granted regular hearings with a Hoodoo medicine man and twice participated in Nine Night ceremonies, a service conducted to prevent the dead rising from their graves.

Much of her time during her last three months in Jamaica was spent with a colony of Maroons, a warrior caste of former slaves who'd fought to obtain their freedom and evaded recapture or assimilation ever since. They lived in Accompong, high up in the lush mountains of St Catherine. Their leader provided a decidedly uncooperative goat as transport to help Hurston reach their remote settlement. Again defying the usual demarcations of gender, Hurston was to accompany the men on a hog hunt deep into the jungle that left her with severely blistered feet.

The most unfortunate incident to befall Hurston in Jamaica, however, was to occur in the island's metropolitan capital. It was while grabbing a quick lunch in a restaurant in Kingston that a wallet containing substantial sums of money and, more unfortunately, the credit note that authorized her to draw on her Guggenheim funds at the city's branch of Barclays Bank was stolen. Left penniless and refused access to her account by officious counter clerks, Hurston had to borrow money to wire New York to obtain an emergency stipend to see her through until a replacement credit note could be sent to her.

Hurston's Time in Jamaica and Haiti

JAMAICA

N

| 0 | 50 | 100 km |
| 0 | 25 | 50 mi |

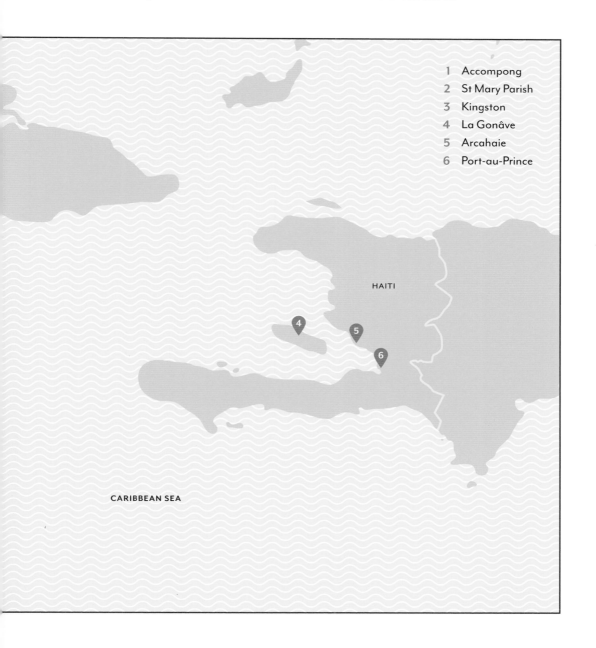

1 Accompong
2 St Mary Parish
3 Kingston
4 La Gonâve
5 Arcahaie
6 Port-au-Prince

HAITI

CARIBBEAN SEA

◀ PREVIOUS PAGE View over
the Blue Mountains towards
Kingston, Jamaica.

As interesting (and infuriating) as she'd found Jamaica, it could not hold a candle to Haiti. Within weeks of arriving back in Port-au-Prince on 23 September, Hurston was already writing to the secretary of the Guggenheim Foundation about the possibility of a second grant to allow her to spend more time gathering information there on its religious practices. If often overwhelmed by the things she saw and heard, and diligently seeking to acquire a solid knowledge of the complex pantheon of voodoo gods and their various whims, and observe the actions of the priests, adepts and devotees at first hand, her thoughts also now turned to the love she'd so unceremoniously left behind. Returning from one particularly long day in the field collecting Haitian stories, exhausted but still feeling restless, she started to write a novel. Feeling remorse for the way she'd ended her affair with Punter, and wishing to explain her need for self-determination, the book recounted the ultimately doomed quest of Janie Crawford, a bright Black woman from Eatonville, for autonomy and a fulfilling romantic life. Written at breakneck pace, in just seven weeks, the book was finished on 19 December. Hurston immediately posted the manuscript of *Their Eyes Were Watching God* to her American publisher and dashed off to spend the Christmas holidays on the island of La Gonâve, slightly to the west of Port-au-Prince.

Coming back to the mainland, she went to Arcahaie and took instruction from one of voodoo's highest priests, the legendary Dieu Donnez St Leger, and supposedly witnessed, among a plethora of other sacraments, the resurrection of a recently dead man, after a sacrifice of pigeons and chickens.

▲ West Queen Street, Kingston, Jamaica, March 1937.

Hurston left Haiti for the United States in early March 1937, and upon arriving in New York learned that her publisher had nothing but praise for her new novel and intended to publish it that autumn. The author, who was also under contract to produce a book about her excursions in the Caribbean for the same company (and that would subsequently be published as *Tell My Horse* in 1938), was anxious to return to Haiti to finish her studies there. Problems with passports were to delay her second visit to Haiti for two months, but once back she renewed her delving into voodoo and the much-contested area of zombies. Having completed these, she sailed back home, landing in New York in late September and discovering *Their Eyes Were Watching God* was the talk of the town. That novel, after a period of neglect and condescension by some male critics, went on to become one of the most significant books in the annals of African-American feminist literature.

◀ Zora Neale Hurston beating the hountar, or mama drum, 1937.

Jack Kerouac Goes on the Road for the First Time

In the summer of 1947, Jack Kerouac (1922–1969), the future figurehead of the Beat Generation of writers and the author of *On the Road*, a novel set to inspire millions to embark on their own freewheeling road trips across America, had been reunited in New York with his old prep school buddy Henri 'Hank' Cru. Cru was en route to San Francisco, where he was to join a ship as its chief electrician. He invited Kerouac to come out west and sign on as his assistant; an opportunity, excuse even, that Jack, scarcely half way through a tortuous draft of his debut novel *The Town and the City*, jumped at.

On 17 July, Kerouac set out from the family home at 133-01 Cross Bay Boulevard, Ozone Park, Queens, and boarded the Seventh Avenue subway line though Morningside Heights and Harlem to its terminus at 242nd Street in the Bronx. From there Kerouac took a streetcar (trolley bus) out to Yonkers. For an author later famed for espousing unfettered free expression and what he termed 'spontaneous prose', a form of writing that attempted to emulate the wild improvisations of bebop jazz musicians, the planning for his trip was precise and meticulous. Kerouac was to map out his route in red pen with an accountant's eye for the potential expenses likely to be incurred.

Since his financial resources were limited, Kerouac calculated on hitch-hiking much of his way to California, and to begin with his luck held. After thumbing a series of rides north along the course of the Hudson River, he landed some 80 kilometres/50 miles north of New York at the entrance to Route 6, where the city quickly gave out to rural Connecticut and the start of the Appalachian Trail. Unfortunately stormy weather meant the roads were empty and Kerouac ended up sheepishly tip-toeing back to New York and Penn Station, where he reluctantly forked out for a Greyhound bus ticket to Chicago. This ride was to be characterized in *On the Road* as 'ordinary' with 'crying babies and hot sun and countryfolk getting on at one Penn town after another, till we got on the plain of Ohio and really rolled, up by Ashtabula and straight across Indiana'.

In Chicago he booked into a cheap room in a YMCA, and hotfooted it to the Loop, a downtown area where some of the city's best jazz joints were located. Quickly moving on, another bus landed him in Joliet, where he succeeded in being picked up by a truck driver who carried the Beat writer to the state line of Illinois. Here he met by chance a middle-aged woman who needed someone to assist with driving her car to Davenport, Iowa, the birthplace of one of Kerouac's heroes, the jazz musician Bix Beiderbecke. This section of the journey afforded the writer his first glimpse of the Mississippi River, which in *On the*

Road he was to maintain smelled 'like the raw body of America itself'.

On 28 July he reached Denver, Colorado, home of his friend Neal Cassady, the free-living former petty crook and jailbird and writer of astonishing letters who was to be immortalized by Kerouac in *On the Road* as Dean Moriarty, and in other writings as Cody Pomeray. Cassady was at this time engaged in a complicated triad of romantic relationships, simultaneously sleeping with his wife Luanne, the poet Allen Ginsberg and his new squeeze and future second wife Carolyn Robinson. Beyond these liaisons he was also holding down a full-time job and so Kerouac saw his spiritual and epistolary soulmate only fleetingly during the few days he spent in Denver.

Within twenty-four hours of arriving in Denver, Kerouac had sent a desperate letter to his mother begging her to wire him $25 for the price of a bus ticket to continue on to San Francisco. He was already broke and surmised that the chances of cadging any lifts across the mountainous and desert terrain of the Rocky Mountains, the Great Basin and the Sierra Nevada were limited to say the least, and dangerous to boot.

When his mother's funds eventually arrived, he took off, observing Salt Lake City and Reno, Nevada, through the window of a bus. After passing through Truckee in California, Kerouac dozed through much of the rest of the journey and had to be roused from his seat when the bus pulled into Market and Fourth Street in San Francisco. After wandering the city's hilly streets, he crossed over the Golden Gate Bridge into Marin County to be reunited with Cru. But instead of the promised job, Cru could only offer Kerouac a position alongside him as a security guard with the Sausalito Police Department, on decidedly meagre pay, although with the perk of getting to wear a badge and uniform and carry a gun and truncheon.

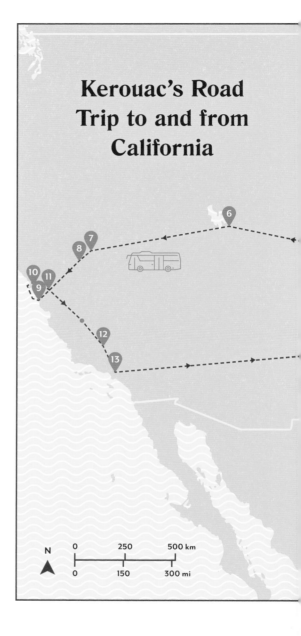

Kerouac's Road Trip to and from California

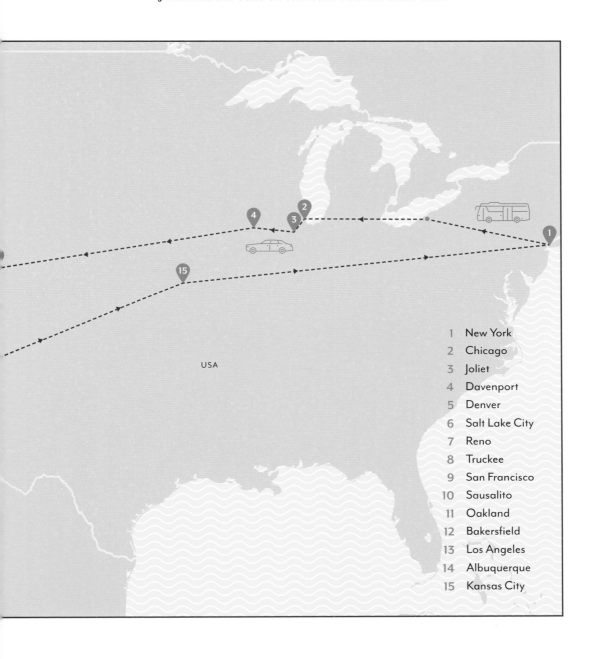

1 New York
2 Chicago
3 Joliet
4 Davenport
5 Denver
6 Salt Lake City
7 Reno
8 Truckee
9 San Francisco
10 Sausalito
11 Oakland
12 Bakersfield
13 Los Angeles
14 Albuquerque
15 Kansas City

USA

◀ PREVIOUS PAGE The Loop, Chicago.

◀ Portrait of Neal Cassady and Jack Kerouac, 1952.

▶ Marin County, California, USA.

By late September, Kerouac had tired of law enforcement and turned in his badge. After climbing Mount Tamalpais, he bid his farewells and set course for the east coast. He was in Oakland by 14 October, and from there coasted the San Joaquin Valley to Bakersfield. Once again failing to find cars receptive to hitch-hikers, he made for the bus station and bought a ticket to Los Angeles. On the bus he met Bea Franco, a young Mexican woman fleeing an abusive husband, with whom he struck up a romantic relationship, the pair at first holing up in a hotel off Hollywood's Main Street and later picking grapes and cotton together to raise sufficient money to resettle in New York. As it was, they parted on a promise that neither of them believed would be kept, that she'd follow him to New York once various family matters were settled. She'd reappear in fiction, at least, as Terry in *On the Road*.

Kerouac sped away once more by bus from Los Angeles to Albuquerque, New Mexico, and Kansas City and from there solidly east until he arrived safely back in New York on 29 October 1947. Though his trip was over, Kerouac's personal journey was really only just beginning, and thousands of miles more would need to be travelled before *On the Road* was ready to be unleashed on an unsuspecting reading public.

▲ Salt Lake City.

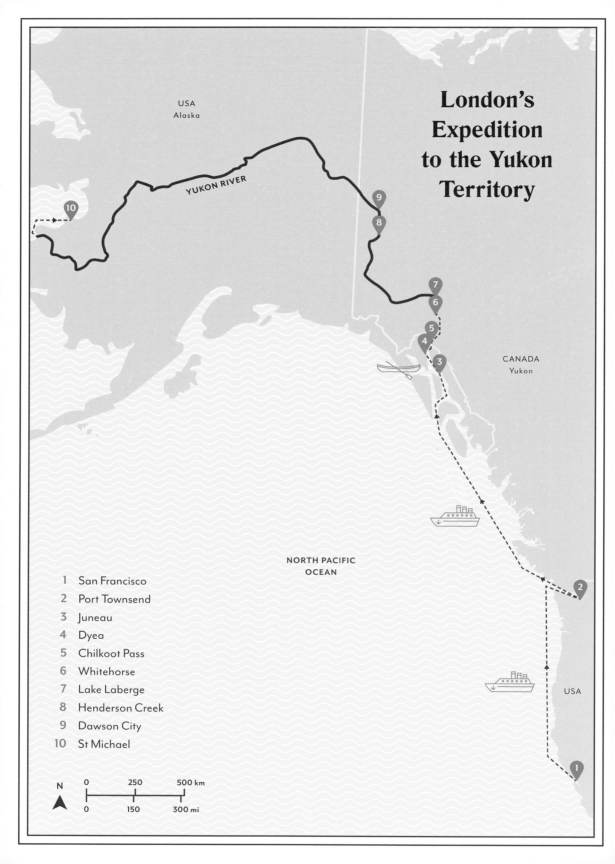

London's Expedition to the Yukon Territory

USA
Alaska

YUKON RIVER

CANADA
Yukon

NORTH PACIFIC
OCEAN

USA

1 San Francisco
2 Port Townsend
3 Juneau
4 Dyea
5 Chilkoot Pass
6 Whitehorse
7 Lake Laberge
8 Henderson Creek
9 Dawson City
10 St Michael

N

0	250	500 km
0	150	300 mi

Jack London Pans for Gold in the Klondike

As Jack London (1876–1916) was later to observe, if he never realized a cent from his brief spell prospecting for gold in the Yukon territory of Canada, the writer managed 'to pan out a living ... on the strength of the trip'. What he saw and heard there was to supply him with a lifetime of stories. Within two years of leaving the Klondike, London became one of the best-paid writers in America, acclaimed as the American Kipling. His most cherished and enduring books, *The Call of the Wild* and *White Fang*, as well as many other novels and works of short fiction, were all to draw closely on his stint in the Yukon.

London was just twenty-one years of age when he became one of an estimated 100,000 (largely) men who struck north upon hearing that gold had been found in the Yukon; a vast, remote, barely inhabited and extremely inaccessible region of Canada comprised of glaciated mountain ranges, lakes and dense spruce forest. Although a comparative youngster, London had already spent the previous eight years variously as a hoodlum, sailor, vagabond wanderer, manual labourer, student and budding journalist. Indeed he attempted, without success, to persuade one of the Californian newspapers he wrote for to fund his excursions into these northern gold fields by hiring him as a special correspondent.

In the event, his sixty-year-old brother-in-law Captain James Shepard, swept up by the gold rush mania dubbed Klondicitis, wanted in, mortgaging (apparently with her consent) his wife's house to bankroll the venture.

In preparation for the arctic conditions they were likely to meet, the pair splashed out on 'fur-lined coats, fur caps, heavy high boots, thick mittens; and red-flannel shirts and underdrawers of the warmest quality'. They also had to purchase mining and camping gear (tents, shovels, axes, blankets, stoves, etc.), and it was a stipulation of the Canadian government that only those carrying a year's worth of food and supplies were allowed to enter their territory. London, in the deal hashed out between the two men, was expected to do the lion's share of lugging all this stuff to the gold fields.

Decked out in their mining duds and laden with their equipment, London and Shepard clambered aboard the *Umatilla* on 25 July 1897 and sailed from San Francisco to Port Townsend, Washington, around 55 kilometres/30 nautical miles north of Seattle. At Port Townsend they joined the *City of Topeka*, another ship loaded with fellow gold-seekers bound for Juneau, Alaska. Making the acquaintance of three like-minded men during the voyage, James 'Big Jim' Goodman, Ira Sloper and

Fred C. Thompson, London and Shepard agreed to form a mining party with them. Unlike many of the fools rushing north with dreams of getting rich quick, Goodman was an experienced miner and hunter; Sloper, if a slip of a fellow, came with skills as a carpenter; and Thompson, a laconic former court clerk, was a methodical organizer, who – to the eternal gratitude of those wishing to separate the fact from London's later fictions – kept a diary charting their course to the Klondike.

Docking at Juneau on 2 August, the party hired Tlingit Native Americans with canoes, and three days later paddled up the 160-kilometre/100-mile-long fjord to Dyea. Here was where the going was destined to get tough as ahead of them now lay the Chilkoot Trail, the brutal uphill mountainous pathway whose zig-zagging course needed to be negotiated to reach the summit of the Chilkoot Pass – the Alaskan border crossing into Canada. Only nine days into their trek, Shepard, already struggling and possibly suffering with a weak heart and rheumatism, threw in the towel and made for home. His place was soon taken by Martin Tarwater, a game old soul they met at Santa Rosa who'd offered to cook, clean and pitch in where required to join the gang. London would later fictionalize Tarwater in his autobiographical story, 'Like Argus of the Ancient Times'.

By the end of the month, they had reached the Chilkoot Pass and were allowed entry into Canada. Now all they had to do was build a boat and navigate a series of lakes and trails to get to the Yukon River. And from there began a 800-kilometre/500-mile journey on its waters north to Dawson City. With the weather already turning wintry, the party was locked into a race against time, needing to reach the Yukon before it froze over and became completely impassable until the following spring.

With the clock ticking, their most fraught decision was to plump to shoot the rapids at Box Canyon and Whitehorse. The foaming chutes of the latter, lying on a tributary of the Yukon known as the Sixty Mile River, were recorded as wrecking at least 150 boats in the next year alone. But with London at the helm, their craft (christened the *Yukon Belle*) cleared Whitehorse with ease, speeding its crew on to Lake Laberge. Though severe north winds and snowstorms would stall their progress here, and it took a week for them to row across the lake, the *Yukon Belle* finally entered the Thirty Mile River – the last tributary before the Yukon itself – on 2 October.

Seven days later, and now only 128 kilometres/80 miles south of Dawson City, they spotted an abandoned but serviceable-looking cabin that had once belonged to the Hudson Bay Company on an island at the mouth of the Stewart River and Henderson Creek. With temperatures dropping and the Yukon already growing slushy, they decided to settle here for the winter. After unpacking and making the 3 x 3.5-metre/10 x 12-foot cabin as habitable as possible, the party even did a little prospecting, Goodman detecting a promising glint in his pan.

While the Yukon was still flowing, London and Thompson were dispatched to Dawson City to file the claim and pick up any news and additional supplies. Fortuitously for London's future literary output, he and Thompson pulled up and camped beside a cabin occupied by Louis and Marshall Bond. Though a pair of Yale graduates and the offspring of one of the wealthiest men in California, Judge Hiram Gilbert Bond, the brothers, who'd initially taken the heavily bearded London for a typical Klondike hobo,

▶ Juneau, Alaska, USA.

were quickly won over by the writer's eloquence and winning personality. The Bond brothers also owned a cross-bred St Bernard and Scotch Shepherd dog named Jack, who was to be the basis for London's Buck, the canine hero of *The Call of the Wild*.

Dawson City was hardly a year old, and in the manner of such places most of its facilities were geared to satisfy the baser appetites of Argonauts. London was to spend most of the six weeks the pair enjoyed in the city haunting the Elkhorn and Eldorado saloons for warmth and company. And also crucially to pump the old-timers for their hard-luck stories of mining life. London, as others noted, was as fine a listener as a conversationalist, and such a personable character that people of all stripes were happy to confide in him.

Eventually, he and Thompson were compelled to go back to Henderson Creek and rejoin their mining partners, undertaking the journey in snowshoes along the frozen Yukon River in bitter sub-zero temperatures. What they returned to was months of forced confinement in cramped, freezing conditions, subsisting on a diet of sourdough bread, beans, bacon grease and gravy – the lack of fresh vegetables in this fare causing all of them to come down with scurvy.

London's generosity with their limited resources caused him to quarrel with Sloper. The final straw came when he broke an axe belonging to the carpenter chopping ice for water and London was forced to move into a neighbouring cabin with three other men. The tensions of this episode were to be conveyed in his short story 'In the Far Country', in which two men stowed up for the winter in a Klondike shack end up killing each other.

When the Yukon thawed in the May of 1898, London and one of his new cabinmates dismantled their house and turned it into a raft to sail down to Dawson City. Selling its logs they raised some $600, and the writer was able to assuage some his symptoms of scurvy by eating raw potatoes and drinking lemon juice. By 8 June, London had decided to quit Dawson. He and two other men left in a small boat, in which they rowed over 2,400 kilometres/1,500 miles down the Yukon River to the Bering Sea. After an exhausting near-month-long journey along the river, they moored at St Michael on the Alaskan Coast at the end of June. Signing on as a coal stoker on a steamer to San Francisco, London was back home in Oakland in late July 1898; his body broken and pretty much flat broke but with a head full of tales to tell and sell for the next eighteen years.

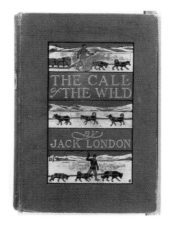

◀ Illustration showing gold seekers crossing the Chilkoot Pass during the Alaskan Gold Rush, 1897.

▶ Front cover of *The Call of the Wild*, 1903.

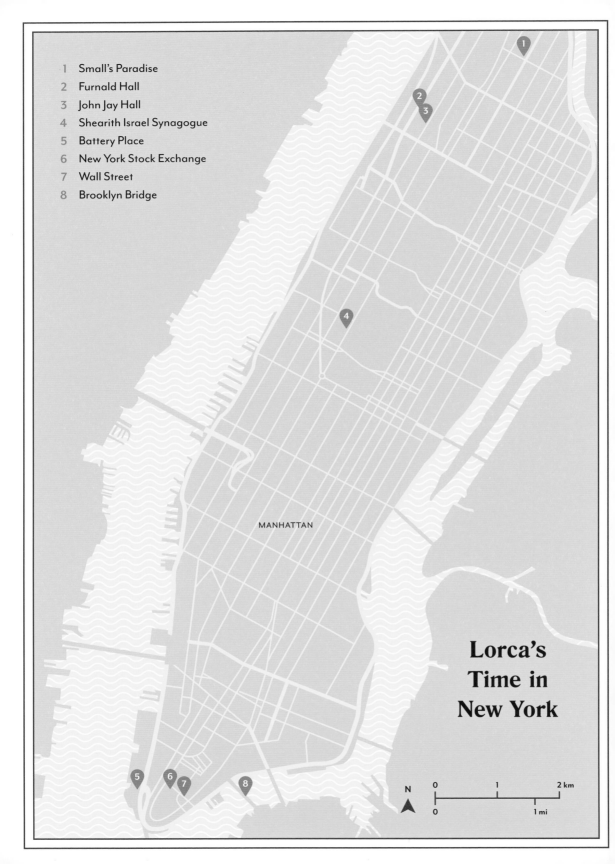

1 Small's Paradise
2 Furnald Hall
3 John Jay Hall
4 Shearith Israel Synagogue
5 Battery Place
6 New York Stock Exchange
7 Wall Street
8 Brooklyn Bridge

MANHATTAN

Lorca's Time in New York

N

0   1   2 km

0   1 mi

Federico García Lorca Takes a Bite of the Big Apple

By the late spring of 1928, Federico García Lorca (1898–1936), the Spanish poet and dramatist and surrealist compadre of Salvador Dalí and Luis Buñuel, had fallen into a state of depression. The acclaim afforded *Gypsy Ballads*, his recently published collection of lyrical verse celebrating the Roma people and the myths, character and colour of his native Andalusia, had made him close to a household name in Spain. But its success strained his relationship with Dalí and he became convinced that Buñuel (among others) was conniving to undermine his friendship with the painter and his reputation in general. Adding to his woes, the object of his greatest affection, the handsome sculptor Emilio Aladrén, with whom he had conducted a probably (sexually) unrequited romance, had become seriously involved with Eleanor Dove, an English woman in the cosmetics trade in Madrid.

Concerned about their son's mental health, Lorca's parents sought advice from some of his friends in Madrid, one of whom suggested that a trip outside Spain might do him some good. Soon after, the poet announced his intention to accompany Fernando de los Ríos, the socialist politician and professor of law who'd adopted Lorca as one his protégés at the University of Granada, to New York, where De los Ríos was to give a lecture at Columbia University.

Lorca's arrival in the United States had been eagerly anticipated in Hispanic literary circles, and the poet found a welcoming party of Spanish acquaintances and journalists waiting for him on the dock when he disembarked on 29 June 1929. Chief among them were Federico de Onis, the chair of Spanish at Columbia, and Angel del Rio, another member of Columbia's Spanish department, later to publish a study on Lorca. De Onis secured the poet university accommodation with a room (number 671) in Furnald Hall on Columbia's Morningside Campus by enrolling him as a student of English. If Lorca was a diligent attender of classes in this course, which was intended to provide foreign nationals with a grounding in the language, his grasp of English was to remain rudimentary at best. Del Rio was to recall that after nine months in America, Lorca largely survived by committing key phrases to memory phonetically and that his pronunciation was appalling.

The city's topography and its easy-to-comprehend gridded layout made New York an incredibly accessible place for the poet. Lorca liked almost nothing more than ambling about its lively streets and walked about constantly, pounding the sidewalks of Harlem, the Battery, the Lower East Side, Broadway and Fifth Avenue and dropping in on jazz clubs, cinemas, musical theatres, diners and speakeasies (Prohibition laws against the consumption of alcohol then still in force). The titles of some of the almost hallucinatory verse he composed in the wake of such perambulations – 'Landscape of a Vomiting Multitude (Coney Island Dusk)', 'Landscape of the Urinating Crowd (Battery Place Nocturne)', 'Unsleeping City

(Brooklyn Bridge Nocturne)' – give a sense of his immersion in and delight and disgust at the seamier sides of the city. The variety of its inhabitants, their ethnic and religious diversity, were further objects of fascination to him. He attended services in Protestant churches, their austere decor and dour rituals only serving to reinforce his love of the spectacle of the Spanish Catholic tradition in which he'd been raised. He found the liturgy and music he heard in the Sephardic synagogue of Shearith Israel on the corner of Central Park West and 70th Street more to his liking.

The poet Hart Crane, with whom Lorca was reputed to have spent a pleasant evening carousing with drunken sailors, was among the American literary acquaintances he made in New York. Another was the novelist and nurse Nella Larsen, whose father was Black and mother white Danish. Larsen introduced Lorca to Harlem, and its Afro-American

churches and its nightclubs. Small's Paradise, in the basement of 2294 Seventh Avenue and one of the district's leading jazz joints, becoming a regular hangout. One of Lorca's earliest poetic responses to New York was 'The King of Harlem', a deeply felt denunciation of the plight of Black Americans and, to his mind, their nation's racist, capitalist system.

While out one night on Broadway, Lorca was to be reunited with an old English friend, Campbell Hackforth-Jones, who he'd previously met in Spain. Hackforth-Jones had been sent by his father, a London stockbroker, to undertake an apprenticeship with an associate's firm on Wall Street. While from then on enjoying many a pleasant night drinking

▼ Small's Paradise nightclub in Harlem, New York, 1929.

▶ View towards the Empire State Building, New York.

contraband gin with Hackforth-Jones and his sister Phyllis at their rented apartment near 70th Street, Lorca was also given a guided tour of the New York Stock Exchange by the Englishman. This exposure to the almost Dionysian exultation of money made flesh duly feeding directly into poems like 'Dance of Death', his freewheeling denunciation of Wall Street financial speculation.

Some months on, Lorca was to join the frantic crowds outside the Stock Exchange following the Wall Street Crash of 29 October 1929, and claimed to have witnessed at least one suicide by a banker hurling himself out the window of a nearby skyscraper and on to the street below.

Before then however, and during the summer recess, Lorca left Manhattan, accepting first an invitation to join the American poet Philip Cummings and his parents at their holiday home beside Lake Eden in the foothills of the Green Mountains in Vermont. These tranquil surroundings and the balm of the natural world helped calm the poet's nerves, which had started to fray in the Big Apple. After ten days in Vermont, Lorca went to join Del Rio and his wife Amelia in their cabin at a farm in Bushnellsville, near Shandaken in the Catskills.

'Poems from Lake Eden Mills' and the sequence 'In the Farmer's Cabin' were to be some of the poems that resulted from this time outside the city.

Lorca returned to New York on 21 September 1929 and moved into room 1231 at John Jay Hall in the heart of Columbia's campus. This was to be his final known address in New York, and it was here that many of the poems that were to be published in his collection *A Poet in New York* were drafted. But it wasn't long before he received an invitation from Instituto Hispano Cubana to lecture in Havana the following spring, a welcome development for the poet since he was by now desperately homesick. Manhattan, as his biographer Ian Gibson has argued, had only made the poet 'appreciate how passionately he loved his native land'. And when he left New York on 4 March 1930 on a train to Tampa, Florida, where he'd board a steamer for Cuba, Lorca, was, as one contemporary commentator astutely noted, arguably 'more Spanish and more Andalusian and more Granadan, than ever'.

▼ Lake Eden, Vermont, USA.

Katherine Mansfield Mines Her Time at a German Spa for Stories

T oday tourists to Bad Wörishofen, the German town in the Bavarian Alps once fashionable as a spa resort, will find a statue of the New Zealand author Katherine Mansfield (1888–1923) standing beside the Iceberg Pond in its Spa Park. She remains one of the most famous visitors to have come here to take the hydrotherapy cure, devised and popularized by the local Catholic priest Sebastian Kneipp. In Mansfield's time, Wörishofen was home to some 3,000 permanent residents but welcomed over 9,000 sickly malingerers annually. The latter coming to avail themselves of Kneipp's treatments, mostly comprised of hosings with ice-cold water, amid the town's serene but sublime alpine scenery.

To a certain extent it's surprising that Mansfield should be granted such an honour, for the writer was to leave an astonishingly caustic portrait of the denizens of Wörishofen in her debut collection of short stories, In a German Pension, published in December 1911. According to her second husband, John Middleton Murry, she refused to allow the book to be republished during the First World War, fearing that her youthful satirical mocking of certain elements of the Germanic character and culinary habits would be seized upon by jingoistic British propagandists.

The collection, for all of its juvenile faults, marked the arrival of a singularly modern writer in her own right. The period of the book's composition

and eventual acceptance for publication was one blighted by sickness, personal tragedy, doomed and desperate romantic encounters and emotional turmoil. If her biographers have managed to roughly surmise most of what occurred during these years, some elements remain contested and attempts to create a fuller picture have been hampered by Mansfield's decision to destroy almost all her correspondence from this time and her 'huge complaining diaries', as she later described them, from 1909–12.

Brought up in New Zealand and partially educated in London, Mansfield was a remarkably free-spirited and sexually liberated young woman who desired both men and women. Returning to London in 1908, she formed an attachment to the violinist Garnet Trowell, whose twin brother she'd also previously been sweet on. After a brief period living in the Trowell household, she departed following a fierce row with Garnet's parents who had raised objections to their relationship. Already three months pregnant by the musician, she promptly accepted an offer of marriage from an older singing teacher, George Bowden, but was to abandon him the morning after their wedding night, having been unable to bring herself to consummate the union. Attempting to rekindle her love affair with Garnet, who was on tour with an operatic company, Mansfield travelled

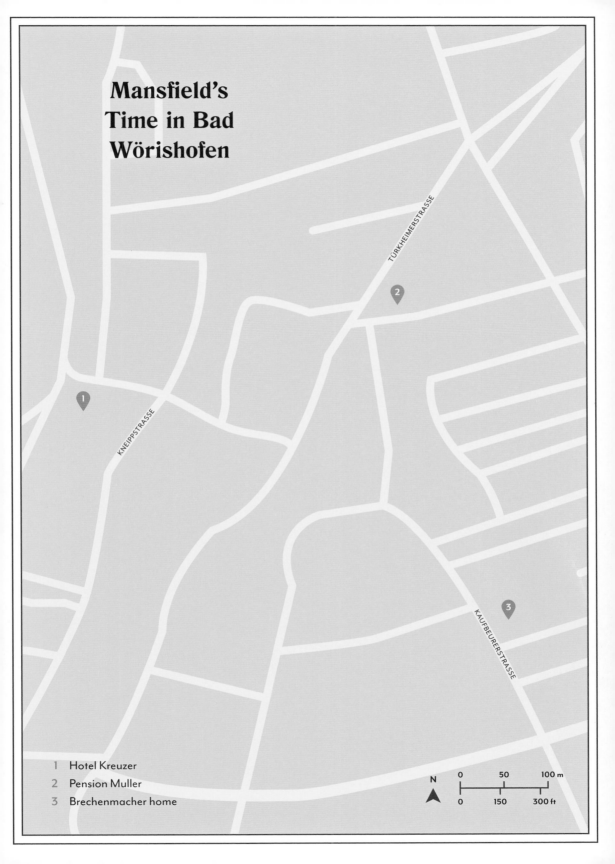

Mansfield's Time in Bad Wörishofen

1 Hotel Kreuzer
2 Pension Muller
3 Brechenmacher home

N

0   50   100 m
0   150   300 ft

◀ Unterallgäu Alps, Bavaria, Germany.

to Liverpool to join him. She was to spend nearly a month on the road with him before concluding it was over between them and making for Bruges in Belgium for a short rest and to reassess her options.

News of the collapse of her hasty marriage and rumours not just of her liaison with Garnet but also of a friendship, verging on the Sapphic, with her London confidante and former college classmate Ida Baker soon reached Mansfield's mother, Annie Beauchamp, in New Zealand. Beauchamp set sail for England, arriving in London on 27 May 1909 to confront her daughter. It was Beauchamp who now spirited her errant child off to Germany. Her reasons for doing so continue be disputed; some biographers doubting whether she was aware of her daughter's pregnancy and others, perhaps more convincingly, arguing that she purposely removed Mansfield to the Continent, where her illegitimate child might be born and put up for adoption far from view of polite British or Kiwi society. In any event, Mansfield was installed in the Hotel Kreuzer on Kneippstrasse in Wörishofen by 4 June, and stayed there for around a week before moving to the cheaper Pension Muller on Türkheimerstrasse. Here she remained for close to the next two months, the boarding house providing the basis for the German pension in her subsequent stories.

According to her biographer Jeffrey Meyers, Mansfield came down with a severe chill after walking barefoot in the nearby forest – an element of the Kneipp treatment regimen – and was left feeling ill, lonely and alienated by her environment; her mother long since having headed back to New Zealand. Such a situation only added acidity to the pen portraits she would write while convalescing. The author was subsequently to find a slightly warmer berth at the home of Fraulein Rosa Nitsch, a woman who ran the lending library out of the post office on Kasinoweg. But after lifting a trunk that was too heavy for her, Mansfield consequently suffered a premature birth to a still-born baby. By late September 1909 she was lodged with the family of Johan Brechenmacher on Kaufbeurerstrasse, where she remained until her final departure in January 1910. The family's surname was destined, however, to live on in her story 'Frau Brechenmacher Attends a Wedding'.

Back in London, Mansfield attempted a short-lived reconciliation with Bowden, moving into his bachelor flat in Gloucester Place, Marylebone, for the next two months. It was Bowden, impressed by the stories she'd written while in Wörishofen, who suggested she send them to *New Age*, a new progressive magazine edited by A.R. Orage. Presented with 'The Child-Who-Was-Tired', Orage immediately agreed to publish it. The story appeared in the 23 February 1910 edition, and a further nine of her stories were to be printed in the journal between then and August. Six months later, *In a German Pension* was to see Mansfield embraced by London's literary meteors, and soon after its publication she was introduced to John Middleton Murry. As the editor of the forward-thinking journal *Rhythm*, Murry became her publisher, as well as in quick succession, her lodger, lover and finally husband. Tuberculosis would alas claim Mansfield at the shockingly youthful age of thirty-four, but arguably she crammed more into the brief time she had than some writers achieve in twice as many decades.

◀ Sebastian Kneipp's rectory in Bad Wörishofen, Germany, c.1890.

▶ Illustration depicting the Kneipp Cure.

KNEIPP CURE.

Fig.1. The Knee-jet.

Fig.2. The Head-affusion.

Fig.3. Walking barefoot in wet grass.

Herman Melville Sees the Watery Parts of the World

'He isn't quite a land animal', D.H. Lawrence once observed of Herman Melville (1819–1891). Lawrence, along with Virginia Woolf, was one of a generation of writers and critics in the first quarter of the twentieth century who championed Melville's work after decades of obscurity and neglect.

Born in New York into a solidly respectable American family of Scots-Dutch extraction, Melville could hardly have predicted the hand fate eventually dealt him. His father, Allan, ran a thriving wholesale business importing fancy wares. This enterprise provided sufficient income to allow the family to live comfortably in a grand house with a fine garden at 675 Broadway, in the fashionable 'Bond Street' district of Manhattan inhabited by genteel professionals. Here Herman and his siblings' education was attended to by a governess. The business also took Melville's father across the Atlantic to obtain stock and cut deals with suppliers and manufacturers in Europe. The young Melville relished hearing his father talk about these travels and relate his impressions of Paris, Bordeaux, London, Liverpool and Edinburgh. The bookshelves of his father's library were crammed with volumes in French and travelogues and guidebooks. Plenty, in essence, to excite the boy's imagination with wild stories and images of far-flung countries. However, when the time came for Melville to undertake an odyssey to the Old World for himself, he would be voyaging not as a prosperous merchant but a common sailor – and of the lowest rank of untrained 'boy' at that too.

Melville was eleven when his father went bankrupt and the family was forced to move up state to Albany, where Melville's maternal grandparents and uncles, aunts and other kin lived. Within two years, his father was dead, leaving his mother, Maria, heavily in debt and with eight children to support. It fell to Melville and his elder brother, Gansevoort, to provide for the family. After spending two years as a trainee clerk in a New York bank, and helping out at his uncle's farm in Pittsfield, Massachusetts, Melville would go on to join Gansevoort in a concern selling furs. But when credit dried up in the Wall Street crisis known as the Panic of 1837, Gansevoort was left bankrupt. Melville then endured an unedifying stint as a teacher in a country school and after that studied a course in engineering. After undertaking a fruitless hunt for a job (almost any job) and having exhausted all other options on dry land, it was only then, two months shy of his twentieth birthday, that Melville turned in desperation to the notion of taking to the oceans.

Melville's comparative youth and lack of sea legs meant he joined the crew of the *St Lawrence* on the

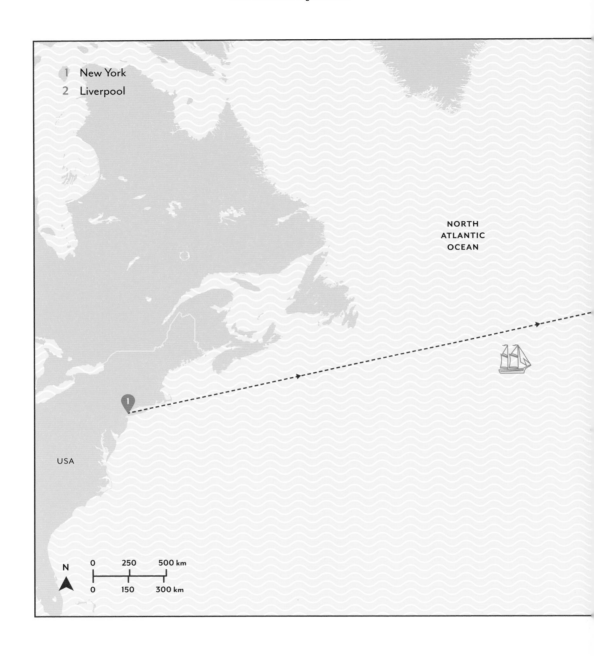

1 New York
2 Liverpool

NORTH
ATLANTIC
OCEAN

USA

N

| 0 | 250 | 500 km |
| 0 | 150 | 300 km |

◀ PREVIOUS PAGE Liver
Building, Pier Head,
Liverpool, England.

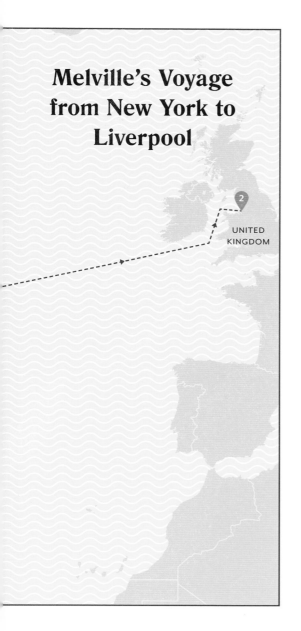

Melville's Voyage from New York to Liverpool

UNITED KINGDOM

bottom rung. The three-masted, square-rigged packet, under the command of Captain Oliver P. Brown, was bound for Liverpool, England. The ship's departure from New York was delayed by an onshore wind and perpetual rain that persisted for three solid days. It was perhaps an ominous portent for a lad whose impractically romantic expectations of this ocean-going escapade had been nourished by his love of Lord Byron's poetry, a notable influence on the juvenile pieces he'd then begun writing. Carrying 920 bales of cotton and a few passengers, the *St Lawrence* finally sailed from Pier 14 on the New York docks on Wednesday 5 June 1837. The official crew list records that a 'Norman Melville (age 19; height 5 ft 8½ in; complexion, light; hair brown)' was aboard – his name most likely mangled by the purser's deciphering of Herman's own, infamously illegible handwriting.

It would be twenty-seven days before the *St Lawrence* reached the River Mersey and fetched up at Prince's Dock. In between Melville had suffered a brutal education in the harsh realities of ship life. As a mere 'boy' he was the dogsbody set to work sweeping and swabbing the decks, slushing masts, coiling rigging and loosing and unfurling sails. He had immediately to learn the names and practical uses of countless ropes and how to tie a bewildering number of knots. It also fell to Melville to stand watches and muck out the ship's pigpen and chicken coops.

He appears to have performed satisfactorily and seems to have taken a certain pride in proving doubters wrong. But he was cut from a completely different cloth to the majority of his crewmates, most of whom were a pretty rough and ready bunch, and he was ribbed mercilessly for his nautical ignorance, bookishness and middle-class manners.

In *Mardi*, Melville's third novel, he appears to offer, as several of the author's biographers have noted, what reads much like a description of his own situation on the *St Lawrence*. He writes:

Now, at sea, and in the fellowship of sailors, all men appear as they are. No school like a ship for studying human nature. The contact of one man with another is too near and constant to favor deceit. You wear your character as loosely as your flowing trowsers. Vain all endeavors to assume qualities not yours; or to conceal those you possess. Incognitos, however desirable, are out of the question. And thus aboard of all ships in which I have sailed, I have invariably been known by a sort of thawing-room title. Not,—let me hurry to say,—that I put hand in tar bucket with a squeamish air, or ascended the rigging with a Chesterfieldian mince. No, no, I was never better than my vocation; and mine have been many. I showed as brown a chest, and as hard a hand, as the tarriest tar of them all. And never did shipmate of mine upbraid me with a genteel disinclination to duty, though it carried me to truck of main-mast, or jib-boom-end, in the most wolfish blast that ever howled.

Whence then, this annoying appellation? For annoying it most assuredly was. It was because of something in me that could not be hidden; stealing out in an occasional polysyllable; an otherwise incomprehensible deliberation in dining; remote, unguarded allusions to Belles-Lettres affairs; and other trifles superfluous to mention.

Ironically, *Mardi* was Melville's first flop; its failure compelled him to bash out in swift succession *Redburn* and *White-Jacket*, two much more straightforward works of maritime fiction that were greeted with sighs of relief by book buyers as a welcome return to earlier form after the overripe philosophizing and convoluted plotting of their predecessor. Melville would always disparage them, though. In one letter, he maintained that they were, 'Two jobs, which I have done for money – being forced into it, as other men are to sawing wood.' But it's doubtful he'd have ever written *Moby-Dick*, his sprawling novel about the peg-legged Captain Ahab's fanatical hunt for the white whale who stole his limb, without having applied himself first to the task of completing these two novels at pace and with such concision. Their sales too, kept him in contention as a publishable proposition. In *Redburn*, finished in just ten weeks, and subtitled 'His First Voyage – Being the Sailor-boy Confessions and Reminiscences of the Son-of-a-Gentleman, in the Merchant Service', he also gave an artfully fictionalized account of his time on the *St Lawrence*. And much as Charles Dickens did with *David Copperfield*, Melville's sailor-boy protagonist, Wellingborough Redburn, shares many elements of his own biography, even down to the loss of a well-travelled, bankrupt, bibliophile father.

The *St Lawrence* was to remain at Liverpool until 13 August. If kept busy with getting the boat ready to make the return journey, the crew were also granted enough leave to explore the city at their leisure. Something Melville, on this his first trip outside the United States, took full advantage of, though lack of money necessarily constrained his experiences of the city and limited his wanderings within it. Liverpool had only fairly recently developed into England's second port. Its rapid and unruly growth was driven by the profits of the transatlantic slave trade and the expansion of the canal network to Lancashire's inland mill towns. Its city fathers rejoiced in their wealth and good fortune. But Melville was shaken by the poverty and beggary he saw in its dockland slums, which he painted at length as a modern-day Sodom and Gomorrah in *Redburn*.

Poor weather was again to intervene with the *St Lawrence*, the packet's westward journey taking forty-seven days and a homesick Melville not making it back to New York until 30 September 1839. His turn at sea had changed him. But he was no wealthier than when he'd left and his family's situation appeared no better either. After a further go as a school teacher, Melville headed for New Bedford, Massachusetts, the 'whaling city' and in January 1841 he departed on the *Acushnet* for the Pacific. Deserting this ship in the following year at the Marquesas Islands in Polynesia, Melville was to accrue a plethora of experiences as a harpooner and mutineer as he drifted from ship to ship from Tahiti to

Hawaii before signing up with the US Navy to secure a homeward passage in 1844.

Encouraged by responses to his reminiscences of his adventures, he wrote them down. The resulting novel, *Typee*, was first printed in Britain in 1846 by the London firm of John Murray – publishers of Byron. And much like his one-time poetic idol, Melville was to wake up and find himself suddenly famous. If alas somewhat fleetingly during his own lifetime.

▼ Engraving of Prince's Dock in Liverpool, England, 1840.

Alexandr Pushkin Convalesces In the Caucasus and the Crimea

Famously the Ancient Greek philosopher Plato banished poets from his ideal city in *The Republic*, fearing the pernicious influence of the wrong kind of verse on its citizens. Almost proving Plato's point, Aleksandr Pushkin (1799–1837), one of Russia's most revered poets, was deemed a serious threat to national security after one of his poems, 'Ode to Freedom', was cited by conspirators of the so-called Decemberist Revolt of 1825. His political poems led to the writer suffering periods of exile, official censorship and coming, more than once, within a hair's breadth of prison and execution.

Precociously making his literary debut aged just fourteen and while still a student at the elite Imperial Lyceum at Tsarskoye Selo, the poet, who on graduating took a post in the foreign office, first fell foul of the Russian authorities six years later. It was then that some of his verses openly mocking Tsar Alexander and attacking rural serfdom came to the attention of the police in St Petersburg. Fortunately influential friends interceded on his behalf and Pushkin avoided a death sentence or expulsion to Siberia, which some considered a fate worse than death.

The poet, after promising to refrain from writing any more political poetry, was transferred to the chancellery of General Ivan Inzov, where it was hoped this seasoned official might instil a proper sense of faith and virtue in the talented but wayward youngster. Inzov was then stationed in the southern Russian city of Dnipro (then Ekaterinoslav) on the Dnieper River in what is now Ukraine. But he was about to be appointed as the plenipotentiary governor of Bessarabia, a role that required the general to move to its provincial capital, Chişinău (Kishinev) in Moldova. And it was here that Pushkin was destined to spend the next three years. Before that, however, Pushkin was to enjoy a brief interlude touring the Caucasus and the Crimea. A sojourn that he later recalled as one of the happiest moments of his life and that was to have a profound effect on his subsequent literary output.

Pushkin's journey south to what he called 'the torrid boundary of Asia' began when he left St Petersburg for Dnipro in the first week of May 1820. After a week of travelling the poet reached Kyiv, where he had arranged to spend the evening with his friend Nikolay Raevsky, a young hussar, and his father, General Nikolay Nikolaevich Raevsky, a decorated military commander. The pair, along with the general's two youngest daughters, were going

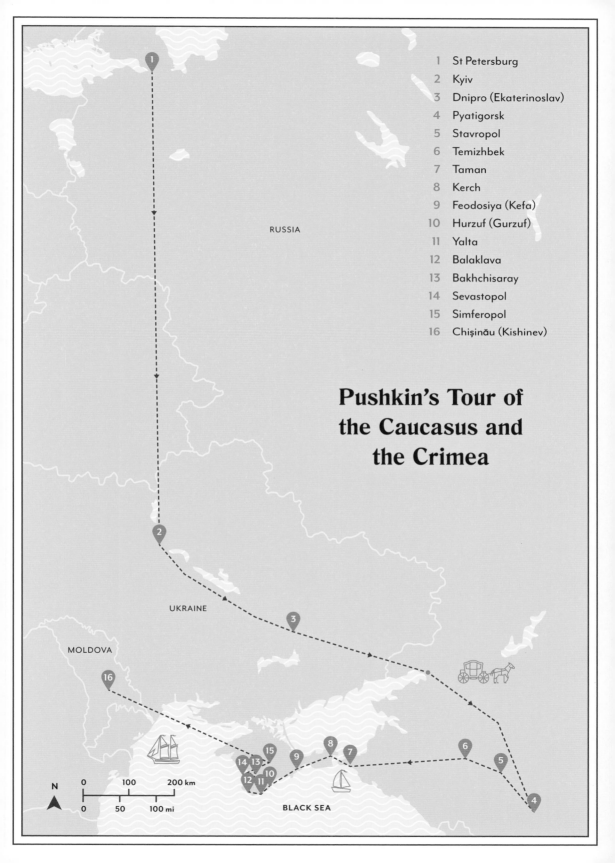

Pushkin's Tour of the Caucasus and the Crimea

1 St Petersburg
2 Kyiv
3 Dnipro (Ekaterinoslav)
4 Pyatigorsk
5 Stavropol
6 Temizhbek
7 Taman
8 Kerch
9 Feodosiya (Kefa)
10 Hurzuf (Gurzuf)
11 Yalta
12 Balaklava
13 Bakhchisaray
14 Sevastopol
15 Simferopol
16 Chişinău (Kishinev)

RUSSIA

UKRAINE

MOLDOVA

BLACK SEA

N

0   100   200 km
0   50   100 mi

to visit the Caucasus, where the general's eldest son, Alexander, was taking the waters at a mineral spa in Pyatigorsk on the slopes of Mount Mashuk. The family and its entourage were then to continue on into the Crimea, joining the general's wife and his two oldest daughters on a jaunt around that part of the country. Since the first leg of this trip would take them through Dnipro, the general agreed to speak to Inzov to ask him if Pushkin might not accompany them on this holiday.

The next morning Pushkin went on ahead to Dnipro. Reaching it three days later, he presented himself to Inov, and seemingly made a favourable first impression on his new boss. Inov, however, was soon preoccupied with the arrangements concerning his new governorship, and the poet was left with little to do. He therefore chose to spend most of his time sailing and swimming and idling about on the riverbank. As a result of all this aquatic activity, though, he came down with a chill. And when the Raevskys reached Dnipro on 26 May, they discovered Pushkin filthy, unshaven and feverish in his rented hovel. General Raevsky succeeded in persuading Inov that Pushkin should spend the summer with the Raevskys for the good of the poet's health (mental and physical), and return to the governor's service in the autumn once Inov was settled in Chișinău.

Travelling in two large carriages and a calash (an open carriage with a folding top), they left Dnipro on 28 May and arrived in Pyatigorsk on 6 June; their route taking them to the shores of the Taganrog Bay, where they all disembarked to admire the Sea of Azov.

At Pyatigorsk, Pushkin was to meet Alexander Raevsky. Just four years older than the poet, Alexander, who was a charming and manipulative man, and a fellow poetic disciple of Lord Byron, was briefly to exert a powerful influence over Pushkin. Their friendship was to sour quite spectacularly, however, over Alexander's duplicity; Pushkin going on

to pen 'The Demon' in 1824, a thinly veiled character assassination of him in verse.

Pushkin and the rest of the adults in the party were to commit themselves to a strict regimen of baths and purges at Pyatigorsk; and they also diligently trailed around other nearby spas in the area. In a letter to his brother, Pushkin would claim that the waters in the Caucasus helped him 'greatly, especially the hot sulphur ones'. The facilities at Pyatigorsk, as elsewhere at this time, remained fairly primitive. The baths, he subsequently remembered, 'were hastily constructed shacks. The spring for the most part ... spouted up, steamed, and flowed down the mountain-side in various directions.' And accessing the water generally involved scaling steep stony paths and clambering along shrub-lined, unfenced precipices. When Pushkin returned to the region some nine years later he was disappointed to find much of this wildness tamed and the spas, if easier to use, far too neat, orderly and prettified to his taste. But then for Pushkin what captivated him most about the Caucasus was the rawness of its scenery and the similarly unvarnished lives of its fascinatingly tribal and predominantly Muslim people. For the young poet it was a place as otherly and exotically alluring, in his biographer T.J. Binyon's opinion, 'as the Levant ... for Byron or the American wilderness ... for Fenimore Cooper'.

On his various excursions around the area, Pushkin sought out Tatar mountain villages on foot or on horseback, and the poet liked nothing more than to pump local inhabitants for stories and legends; the taller the better. In one village he supposedly met an old soldier who told him a story

◀ The Crimean coastline and
the Black Sea, Ukraine.

about being held captive by Caucasian bandits, this tale providing him with the basis for one of his most popular poems, 'The Caucasian Prisoner'.

In August, the company left the Caucasus for the Crimea. This journey, after Stavropol, was to take them through lands deemed so potentially hostile that they voyaged with a military escort of sixty Cossacks and a primed cannon. Charting a course through Temizhbek to Taman on the Black Sea, they were to suffer a horrific storm-tossed nine-hour crossing to Kerch, the Ancient Greek Crimean city of Panticapaeum, famed as the site of King Mithridates' suicide. Pushkin had expected to see the ruin of the tomb of Mithridates and traces of Panticapaeum but was confounded to encounter only 'a heap of stones and rough-hewn rocks in the cemetery on the adjacent mountain ... and a few steps' that might have been 'a tomb or the foundations of a tower'. He picked a flower, which he intended to keep as a memento, but ended up losing it 'without the least compulsion' the next day.

From Kerch, they went on to the port of Feodosiya (then Kefa). Here they boarded a naval brig put at the general's disposal, and set sail via the southern shores of the Crimea for Hurzuf (Gurzuf). It was on this ship that Pushkin began composing his first Crimean poem, a romantic elegy. And his first glimpse of Hurzuf, with its multicoloured mountains that 'shimmered brightly', Tatar huts 'like beehives', poplar trees 'like green pillars' and the enormous Mount Ayu-Dag, was to be an image he returned to again and again in verse and prose.

In Hurzuf, he bathed in the sea, gorged on grapes and visited the ruins of a fort constructed by Emperor Justinian I on the nearby cliffs. But also with Nikolay, he readily dipped into volumes held in the library at the house the Raevskys had rented from a

distinguished French émigré, whose book collection ranged from Voltaire to Byron. It was works by the latter in Gallic prose translations that Pushkin read most assiduously during his stay here.

No doubt partly fuelled by the romanticism of Byron's verse and the dramatic Crimean scenery, Pushkin became infatuated with the general's eldest daughter, the striking twenty-two-year-old Yekaterina, and sought, without luck, to woo her. She is widely believed to have been the model for his characterization of the ambitious Russian noble woman Marina Mniszech in his historical tragedy *Boris Godunov*.

After three weeks in Hurzuf, Pushkin, the general and Nikolay embarked on a last tour of the region before their departure. They visited Yalta and Balaklava. In the latter, the St George Monastery, a Christian cave church carved into the rocks of Cape Fiolent by Greek merchants, and the ruins of a temple to Diana were to leave lasting impressions on Pushkin. Before finishing up in Simferopol via Sevastopol, they stopped at Bakhchisaray, where they explored the decaying remains of the sixteenth-century palace of Crimean Tatar Khans, and Pushkin saw a crumbling fountain that he would memorialize in his poem 'The Fountain of Bakhchisaray'. A few days later, Pushkin was away off to Chişinău, but the south and what he called this 'meridional shore' was 'to exert such an inexplicable fascination over' him for the remainder of his days.

◀ *View of Mount Ayu-Dag*, Nikanor Chernetsov, c.1836.

▲ Portrait of Alexander Nikolayevich Raevsky, c.1820.

J.K. Rowling Gets a Train of Thought on the Line from Manchester to London

The story of how an unemployed single mother with a seemingly unpublishable children's book became one of the bestselling authors in the world could almost be a fairy tale. But if touched by magic, the rags-to-riches journey of J.K. Rowling (b. 1965), from a struggling would-be writer to the famed creator of Harry Potter and a household name, was as much down to persistence and hard graft as anything. Yet there is something rather enchanting that of all the places for inspiration to strike, Rowling first had the idea for her boy wizard while on a train. And a rather humdrum one at that, quite unlike the huffing, puffing Hogwarts Express.

In 1990, Rowling was working in London doing various largely temporary office and secretarial jobs, including a spell at a publisher where she had to send out rejection letters to authors whose manuscripts had failed to make the grade. When she was not working (and sometimes even when she was, since she used any office downtime to write), Rowling toiled on a couple of novels for adults.

Her boyfriend at this time was living in Manchester in the north-west of England, a situation that resulted in Rowling regularly taking the train from Euston Station to see him at weekends. This arrangement was far from ideal for either party, and the boyfriend tried to persuade Rowling to get a job in Manchester and move in with him up there. She eventually agreed and would wind up working at the Manchester Chamber of Commerce and later Manchester University, though once again in unfulfilling secretarial roles. Before this, however, the couple needed to find somewhere to live together. And it was after a particularly frustrating weekend of flat-hunting, and having been shown a slew of unsuitable properties by shiny-suited estate agents, that a tired, weary and fed-up Rowling boarded a train at Manchester Piccadilly Station to take her back to London, where a room in a shared flat above a sports shop in Clapham Junction and another early Monday morning start and a day in an office in the city awaited her.

To make matters worse, the train, which would normally take around two and half hours, was severely delayed, and it was to be some four hours before it pulled into Euston Station. But that delay proved to be a godsend. Sitting in the motionless carriage, Rowling was staring out of the window at some grazing cows when an image of Harry Potter, a small boy with green eyes and cracked round

Rowling's Train Journey from Manchester to London

ENGLAND

N

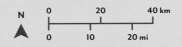

1 Manchester Piccadilly Station

2 London Euston Station

glasses sprung into her head unbidden but almost fully formed. Within an instant she saw him travelling to a boarding school for wizards. As more ideas flooded in, she rummaged in her bag to find a pen to jot them down and to her horror she found there was nothing, not even an eyeliner pencil, to write with inside it. She later confessed she 'was too shy to ask anyone for one on the train'. But the lack of a pen she subsequently believed was for the best because it gave her the remainder of the lengthy journey to think up more ideas for the book. As the train lurched into motion and began its staggered progress through Cheshire, Staffordshire, Northamptonshire,

Buckinghamshire and Hertfordshire, Ron Weasley, Hagrid, Peeves and company and the Hogwarts School of Witchcraft and Wizardry danced into life. Rowling was not to get to put pen to paper until she was finally back in Clapham and she has stated that 'the first bricks of Hogwarts were laid' in that flat.

Five years were to pass, nevertheless, before Rowling finished *Harry Potter and the Philosopher's Stone*, and a further two would pass before it was published and in the bookshops. In all that time, Rowling continued to write, her dedication and determination not only driving her on to complete her first draft but to finish the whole sequence of Harry

◄ Passenger train passing through countryside near Manchester, England.

▲ Platform 9¾, King's Cross Station, London.

Potter books once they'd become so successful, when lesser writers could have buckled under the enormous pressure to provide such follow-ups.

Another much-cherished element of the Harry Potter books, the famous Platform 9¾ at King's Cross Station, from which the Hogwarts Express departs, can also be traced back to her train journeys to Manchester. In an interview with the BBC in 2001, Rowling admitted mixing up King's Cross Station with Euston. 'I wrote Platform 9¾', she told them, 'when I was living in Manchester, and I wrongly visualized the platforms, and I was actually thinking of Euston, so anyone who's actually been to the real platforms 9 and 10 in King's Cross will realize they don't bear a great resemblance to the platforms 9 and 10 as described in the book. So that's just me coming clean, there. I was in Manchester; I couldn't check.'

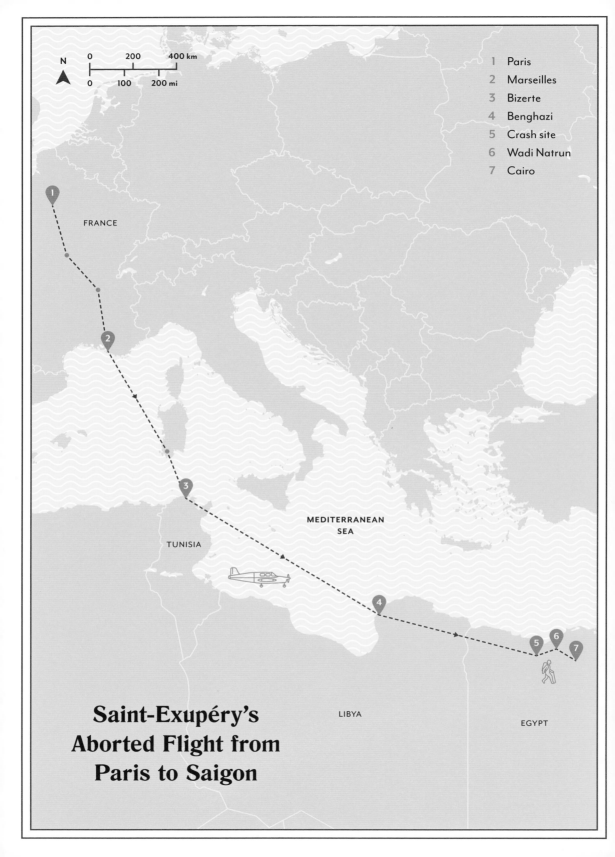

N

| 0 | 200 | 400 km |
| 0 | 100 | 200 mi |

1 Paris
2 Marseilles
3 Bizerte
4 Benghazi
5 Crash site
6 Wadi Natrun
7 Cairo

FRANCE

TUNISIA

MEDITERRANEAN
SEA

LIBYA

EGYPT

Saint-Exupéry's Aborted Flight from Paris to Saigon

Antoine de Saint-Exupéry Crashes into the Headlines

Antoine de Saint-Exupéry (1900–1944), the author of the children's classic *The Little Prince* and pioneering aviator, had initially expressed only scepticism about what *Le Figaro* called '*L'aviation sportive*' (sport aviation) and what were more generally known in French flying circles as 'raids'. These were flights of endurance and adventure, conducted against the clock with the aim of besting earlier records of speed or distance in aeroplanes that often still gave the appearance of being unsuited to prolonged (or indeed, any) spells in the air. But towards the end of 1935, Saint-Exupéry, who'd so far deemed such contests de trop and saw more nobility and genuine purpose in his aeronautical career as a commercial pilot specializing in the carrying of mail, was at a financial low ebb. In addition, his marriage to the Salvadoran writer and artist Consuelo Suncín de Sandoval was going through another stormy patch, her free spirit and fiery temperament and his infidelities once again compounding difficulties, emotional and creative. As a result, when his friend and fellow aviator Jean Mermoz and General René Davet, a high-ranking official in the air force, proposed he enter a French air ministry competition to win 150,000 francs for recording the fastest flight between Paris and Ho Chi Minh City (Saigon) in Vietnam (then part of French-controlled Indochina),

he accepted without hesitation. But his commitment to their plan was half-hearted at best and with a deadline of 31 December 1935 looming, the odds were against them from the start.

While Charles Lindbergh had fretted for months over the precise set of emergency kit to pack on his famed first transatlantic flight in 1927 and André Japy, then the holder of the Paris–Saigon record, had undertaken a series of warm-up flights to Oslo, Oran and Tunis in preparation for his Saigon 'raid', Saint-Exupéry was mostly distracted by his domestic situation. With barely two weeks to go, the poet-writer-pilot had put most of his trust in his Caudron Simoun plane, which with its 180 horsepower engine was a far superior aircraft than that flown by Japy. He confidently, almost insouciantly, predicted being able to shave nearly twenty hours off Japy's ninety-eight hour and fifty-two minute record. The plane's refit for such a journey was undertaken by Davet and his Air Bleu mechanics, with almost no involvement from Saint-Exupéry. And matters of compass readings and mapping of the route were similarly left to Jean Lucas, another Aéropostale colleague.

Saint-Exupéry's companion for the journey was to be one of his most loyal lieutenants, André Prévot, an ex-Air Bleu hand and mechanic and navigator. And their base of operations was the Hôtel Pont Royal in

Saint-Germain-des-Prés, where Saint-Exupéry is said to have spent nearly as long rowing with Consuelo as consulting charts and discussing the mission.

Although official weather forecasts and a prediction by a fortune teller Saint-Exupéry consulted after a send-off dinner at a bistro in Montmartre were decidedly gloomy, the author and Prévot were aloft and on their way by 7.01 a.m. of Sunday 29 December 1935. Their departure was headline news, the public's appetite for stories about continent-spanning aeronauts like Lindbergh unabated. The writer had himself signed an exclusive contract with the Paris paper *L'Intransigeant* to provide a series of articles charting their adventures.

Of the many important decisions taken prior to their departure, perhaps none was more significant than their eschewing a radio in favour (in terms of weight) of additional fuel. As it was, by early on the morning of 30 December when Saint-Exupéry got into difficulty, there was no one he could call upon to confirm his position or radio for help. After flying blind for several minutes and believing himself to be well clear of the Nile, he descended, only to stove into a sand dune in the Egyptian desert at a speed of 273 kilometres/170 miles per hour. Fortunately both Saint-Exupéry and Prévot were able to clamber out of the cockpit almost completely unscathed and the plane didn't explode, allowing the men to retrieve what pitiful rations and supplies they had from the wreckage. Their situation, as the author subsequently reported with masterly French aristocratic understatement, 'was hardly ideal'.

▶ Dunes of the Great Sand
  Sea, Siwa Oasis, Egypt.

Saint-Exupéry and Prévot had crashed about 201 kilometres/125 miles west of Cairo but had absolutely no idea where they were. As Saint-Exupéry's biographer Stacy Schiff points out, if they'd only managed to keep in the air and on course they would most likely have beaten Japy's record as they were a good two hours ahead of schedule at the time of the crash. But none of that was of the slightest importance now. New Year's Eve and the deadline for the prize passed, with the two men parched and completely disoriented, blindly stumbling over the rolling dunes hoping to reach Cairo. Encountering nothing but desert, they tracked back and thankfully changed direction, heading off to the north-east, where at last, on the fourth day, they ran into a Bedouin caravan. The pair were promptly conveyed to the home of Monsieur and Madame Raccaud at Wadi Natrun.

After the airmen had been restored to something closer to life with cups of tea and whisky, Raccaud offered to drive them to Cairo. This stage of the journey, however, proved to be almost farcical. The car ran out of petrol about 6 kilometres/4 miles from the Pyramids. Once more fuel had been acquired, the party stopped at a hotel bar in Giza, some 24 kilometres/15 miles outside Cairo so that Saint-Exupéry could ring the French authorities and let them know he was safe. But the official who took the call, which came after midnight and with a hubbub of drinkers in the background, initially took it to be a prank.

When they reached Cairo, Raccaud dropped the ragged, sunburned pair off at the entrance to the Hotel Continental while he went to park his car. The doorman, officious to a fault, refused to let the men into the hotel, believing them to be beggars. By

◀ Antonie de Saint-Exupéry's Caudron Simoun plane after an emergency landing in the Egyptian desert, 30 December 1935.

▶ André Prévot and Saint-Exupéry posing in front of their plane before departing for their Paris–Saigon flight, Paris-Le Bourget airport, France, 29 December 1935.

chance an international conference of surgeons was then being held in Cairo and at this moment the delegates were returning from dinner and overheard the commotion. Within minutes Saint-Exupéry and Prévot, whose disappearances had been dominating the news since 1 January, had been recognized and were immediately escorted in. Not only did they receive a lavish reception, once bathed, fed and plied with more whisky, their bruised and battered bodies were inspected for any lasting damage by some of the most eminent doctors in the world.

When Saint-Exupéry's call to say they were alive and well came through to the Hôtel Pont Royal in Paris, late on the evening of 2 January 1930, the whole lobby erupted in cheers and celebrations went on into the small hours.

Perhaps even more miraculous than their survival and safe return, was the moving, poetic chronicle of their ordeal and deliverance that Saint-Exupéry was to write, first as a batch of six pieces for *L'Intransigeant*, and then reproduced with minor refinements in *Wind, Sand and Stars*, a book that many continue to view as his finest.

Sam Selvon
Sails to England

The arrival of the *Empire Windrush* at Tilbury Docks in Essex, England, on 22 June 1948 has come to be seen as a pivotal moment in British post-war history. The ship's name itself becoming synonymous with a whole generation of migrants from the British Commonwealth encouraged to settle in Britain throughout the 1950s and 1960s and recruited to fill vacancies in state-run services like the National Health Service and London Transport. Raised to believe that England was the 'Mother Country', these new arrivals, nevertheless, often encountered less than warm welcomes upon reaching the UK. Some suffered appalling racial prejudice in this period and beyond, and struggled to find decent accommodation or work commensurate with their education or abilities.

Trindad-born writer Samuel Selvon (1923–1994) was one such migrant who, having made the journey from the sun-drenched Caribbean to the grey, damp English capital, quickly discovered that the once beating heart of the British Empire could be quite a chilly heartless place for newcomers from its former colonies. The verisimilitude of Selvon's output stems from his own experience and first-hand observations. As the critic Sukhdev Sandhu has, rightly, claimed, 'nowhere do such migrants exist more vividly than in the work of Samuel Selvon'. From the publication of *The Lonely Londoners* in 1956 (the first novel by a Caribbean writer wholly narrated in Creole idioms and speech patterns), the author would chart the travails of the burgeoning Black community in Britain in a series of outstanding stories and novels for the next twenty years. And with the director Horace Ove, he would also provide the script for one of the first British West Indian films, *Pressure*, in 1975.

Selvon was born in 1923 in Mount Moriah Road in San Fernando, a semi-rural city in southern Trinidad. In 1940 he enlisted as a wireless operator in the British Royal Naval Reserve and, encouraged by one of his more bookish naval colleagues, began writing short stories in the downtimes during his long dull shifts. After the war he got a job on the *Trinidad Guardian* in Port of Spain, and between 1946 and 1950 he edited the literary pages of its sister paper, the *Sunday Guardian*. This role saw him becoming acquainted with a formidable crop of emerging young Caribbean writers, among them Derek Walcott, George Lamming and V.S. Naipaul. Selvon's own stories now also began to be published in *Bim*, one of the foremost literary journals in the West Indies, and were broadcast on BBC Radio, one of the few establishment outlets then actively seeking contributions from non-white writers.

Feeling that he needed to go to London to fulfil his literary ambitions, Selvon booked his passage

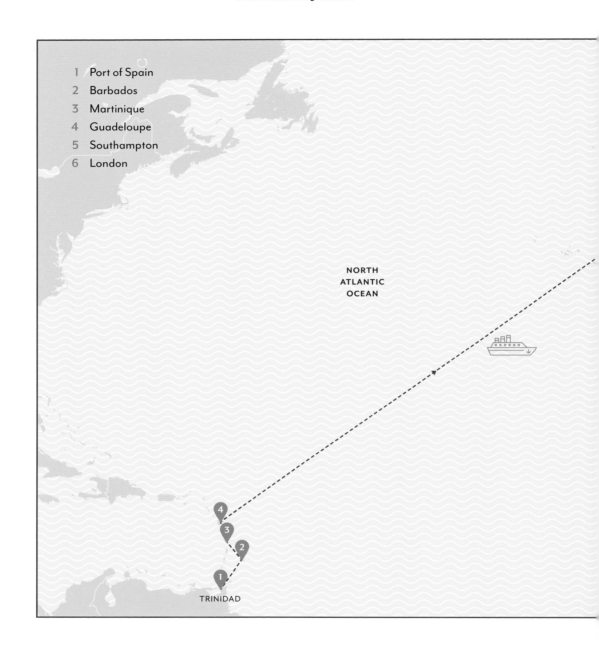

1 Port of Spain
2 Barbados
3 Martinique
4 Guadeloupe
5 Southampton
6 London

NORTH
ATLANTIC
OCEAN

TRINIDAD

◀ PREVIOUS PAGE

Martinique.

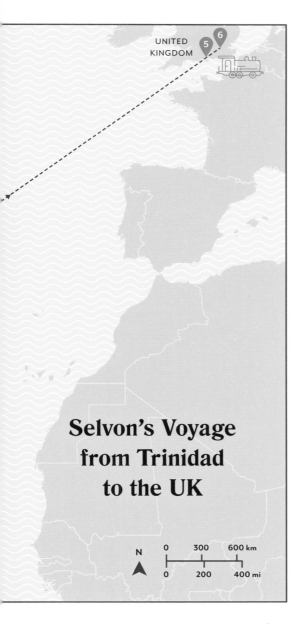

Selvon's Voyage from Trinidad to the UK

UNITED KINGDOM

N

| 0 | 300 | 600 km |
| 0 | 200 | 400 mi |

on a ship sailing for England in mid-March 1950. Unbeknown to him, Lamming was to be travelling on the same boat; and later that year Naipaul was also to leave Trinidad for Britain in order to take up a scholarship at Oxford.

Naipaul, whose fares were covered by the British Council as part of their sponsorship of his education, was to journey in some style; flying to New York with Pan American World before sailing to Southampton on board a transatlantic ocean liner with a first-class cabin all to himself. Though he only acquired his luxurious berth because the ship's purser had not been expecting a 'coloured' passenger. Fearful of asking any of the other all-white tourists if they'd be prepared to share a cabin with him, he resolved the issue by simply bumping the future winner of the Nobel Prize for Literature up to first class.

By contrast, Selvon and Lamming spent nearly a month on what was effectively a French troop carrier. Their vessel was a brutally primitive affair, charting its way to Britain via Barbados, Martinique and Guadeloupe. Only its most affluent white voyagers were accommodated in cabins. Selvon and Lamming were billeted with other West Indian emigrants in a large dormitory lined with metal bunk beds. Their fare was £50 – roughly the equivalent of about £1,000 today – but for the period considered comparatively good value for money.

At the time of the voyage, Selvon already had the working draft of what would become his first novel, the Trinidad-set *A Brighter Sun*, with him. He and Lamming would compete for access to the ship's Imperial typewriter to continue their writing over the course of the journey. Both found the talk of their fellow passengers stimulating, the majority young West Indians seeking to better themselves and possibly make a buck or two into the bargain.

Their first glimpse of Britain was hardly encouraging. As Lamming was later to recall, a

punishing wind rebuffed any attempts to gaze at the approaching landscape. Anchoring in Southampton, Lamming remembered that it dawned on both writers that neither of them possessed return tickets. Clambering on to the train for Waterloo Station in London, the atmosphere became more carnivalesque, with Calypso songs sung and comic stories exchanged and seasoned returnees spelling out the lay of the land for West Indian first-timers.

Genuine anxiety was to grip the party once they reached the London railway terminus as the bulk of these immigrants had no accommodation arranged. Selvon and Lamming were comparatively fortunate; they were to be dispatched by officials from the British Council to the Balmoral Hotel in Queen's Gate Gardens, South Kensington – a hostel routinely recommended as a first port of call for colonial students. There they were to be crammed into 'a

room the size of a successful publisher's office', as Lamming maintained, and as a trio with another new arrival from Africa.

The extraordinary cosmopolitan melting pot that was London was to provide Selvon with his métier. Finding it hard, initially, to make a living from his writing alone, he was employed variously as a cleaner in parts of Bayswater and a clerk at the Indian High Commission and drifted from dismal flat to dismal flat in then ill-regarded parts of West London, long since gentrified. All of which was to find its way into his fictions, providing some of the most lasting portraits of a nascent multicultural Britain and the transition from colonialism in the Caribbean.

▲ Traffic on Westminster Bridge, London, 1949.

▶ A group of West Indian immigrants at Southampton docks, England, 1956.

Bram Stoker Stakes Out Dracula in Whitby

Writers are often asked where their ideas come from. It's a question that by all accounts many dread, as much because there is rarely a simple answer. But what better answer could there possibly be for the inspiration for *Dracula*, that classic chiller with its blood-sucking Transylvanian vampire, than that it was triggered by a disturbing dream: an unholy vision of neck-biting sirens and a gruesome old count that Bram Stoker (1847–1912) jotted down in his notebook on 14 March 1890 with a view to potentially turning it into a story.

A contemporary and friend of Oscar Wilde, Stoker had abandoned a career in the civil service in Ireland to become the 'faithful, loyal and devoted servitor' to the famed actor Henry Irving in London in 1878. It has long been noted that the nocturnal life that Stoker and Irving subsequently led in the theatre and their professional relationship (the former acting as business manager, factotum and enabler to the self-centred, obstreperous and demanding Irving) both have parallels to the two of the main characters in *Dracula*: the eager estate agent Jonathan Harker and the hypnotic vampire himself.

From 1881 onwards, Stoker had been writing fantastical adventure stories, 'most of them execrable' as one literary scholar bluntly puts it. But then in 1890 came his nightmare, and he started mulling over a tale about a vampire he initially, and somewhat reductively, called Count Wampyr. That July, exhausted after completing a theatrical tour of Scotland with Irving,

Stoker took a holiday in Whitby on the North Yorkshire coast. This picturesque fishing village, stacked on the east and west cliffs either side of the River Esk, its two halves connected by a swivel bridge that allowed boats to pass through, had become favoured as a quieter alternative to its neighbour Scarborough.

Whitby possesses regal crescents (Stoker took lodgings at a guest-house on 6 Royal Crescent run by a Mrs Veazey), quaint fishing cottages, a working harbour, sandy beaches and ample points to drink in the sweeping views of the North Sea. Its environs are dominated by the looming overhead presence on the East Cliff of the Gothic ruins of an eleventh-century abbey, an institution erected on the site of a far earlier monastery destroyed by the Danes in 867. Beside the ruins is the graveyard and ancient parish church of St Mary's, which one guidebook from Stoker's time described as 'an ecclesiastical curiosity'. Adding that, 'The ugliness of exterior should not daunt visitors from an inspection of the interior, which is even uglier, but worth seeing on that very account.'

Most probably echoing Stoker's own views, Mina Murray in *Dracula* declares the churchyard 'the nicest spot in Whitby for it lies right over the town ... There are walks, with seats beside them, through the churchyard; and people go and sit there all day long.' One of those seats, and the 199 steps needed to scale the East Cliff to reach it, were to reappear in crucial sequences of the novel.

During his sojourn in Whitby, Stoker is known to have grilled the neighbourhood salts for their stories about shipwrecks and nautical superstitions, which is possibly where he first heard about the *Dmitry*, a Russian schooner wrecked and beached there in a storm in 1885. Though he's also likely to have seen a sepia-print picture of the boat in its prone state on the sands taken by the photographer Frank Meadow Sutcliffe. This vessel would be turned into the fictional *Demeter* – the craft which carries Dracula and his boxes of Transylvanian earth from the Black Sea to Britain, and which washes up at Whitby with only the corpse of its captain lashed to the wheel to show for its crew. Their ghastly fate is revealed in the ship's log, one of a slew of epistolary devices (journals, letters, diaries, etc.) that Stoker uses to relate the novel and heighten its suspenseful action. The contents of that log and accounts of the wrecking of the *Demeter* and Dracula's arrival on these shores in the form of an immense dog that bounds from the bow of the ship and that promptly vanishes after running up into the churchyard, are themselves relayed via newspaper cuttings supposedly pasted into Mina's journal.

By Stoker's standards, *Dracula* was to have an extremely protracted gestation, taking him six years to complete and not published until 1897. Parts of it were written in Cruden Bay in Scotland, where Stoker and his family spent several summers in the 1890s. His widow, Florence, was to recall that it was on this 'lonely part of the east coast of Scotland' that Stoker 'seemed to get obsessed with the spirit of the thing' sitting for hours 'like a great bat, perched on the shore ... thinking it out.'

Stoker's Stay in Whitby

1 West Cliff
2 Whitby Sands
3 Mrs Veazey's guest-house
4 Whitby's Museum and Subscription Library and Warm Bathing Establishment
5 St Mary's Church
6 Whitby Abbey
7 East Cliff

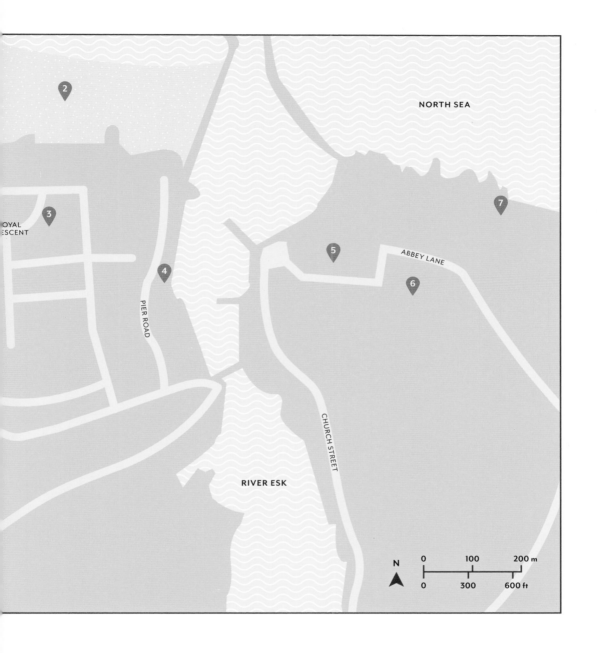

NORTH SEA

ROYAL
CRESCENT

PIER ROAD

ABBEY LANE

CHURCH STREET

RIVER ESK

N

| 0 | 100 | 200 m |
| 0 | 300 | 600 ft |

◄ PREVIOUS PAGE Whitby,
England.

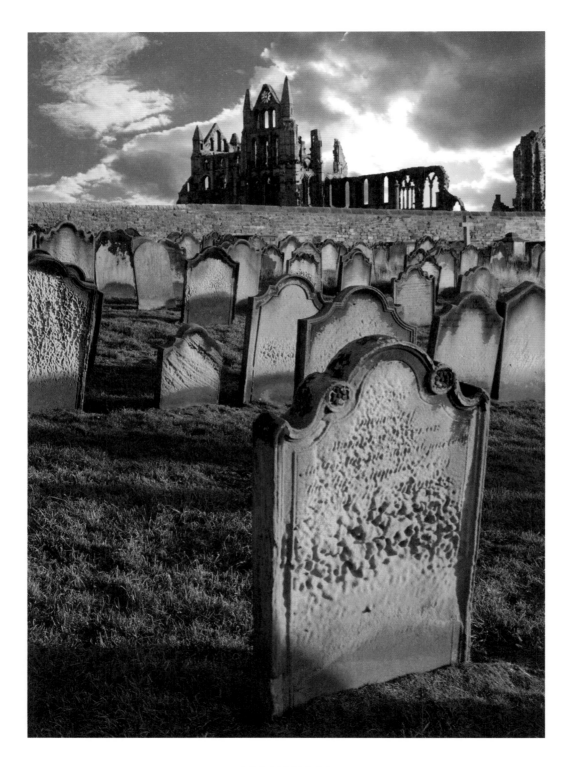

Stoker never made it to Transylvania. But Whitby would stir his imagination and provide the backdrop to many of the book's most gripping chapters, together with supplying its author with several vital pieces of his fictional schema, not least its title and the name of its malevolent lead. For it was in Whitby's Museum and Subscription Library and Warm Bathing Establishment at the Coffee House End of the Quay in August 1890 that Stoker unearthed a copy of the *Account of the Principalities of Wallachia and Moldavia* by William Wilkinson. This memoir by the 'Late British Consul Resident at Bukorest' of his experiences in what is now Romania, published in 1820, was to be a treasure trove of information about the lore and landscape of the Carpathian Mountains. It also had plenty to say about the appalling state of the region's roads.

Stoker was to put chunks of it directly into the mouth of his daylight-shirking count. Most significantly, it was in this book that Stoker read about the fearsome fourteenth-century ruler Vlad III of Wallachia (also known as Vlad Tepes, Vlad the Impaler and Dracula). As Wilkinson recorded, the name Dracula 'in the Wallachian language means Devil' and he maintained that the name was given 'as a surname to any person who rendered himself conspicuous either by courage, cruel actions, or cunning'. Stoker duly, and sensibly, scrubbed out 'Count Wampyr' in the notes for his novel in progress, replacing them with 'Count Dracula'.

◄ Whitby Abbey with gravestones at sunset.

▼ Wreck of Russian schooner *Dmitry*, stranded at Whitby, England, 1885.

Sylvia Townsend Warner Finds Poetry in the Essex Marshes

The Italian author Italo Calvino once maintained that all maps presuppose the idea of a journey. And for Sylvia Townsend Warner (1893–1978) the purchase of one particular map in the summer of 1922 was to lead to an excursion with quite life-changing consequences. As she later wrote, some 'domestic need' had taken her on a day in July into 'the cheap section' of Whiteley's, a London department store not far from her flat on the Queen's Road (now Queensway), Bayswater. Here there was usually a table that displayed bargain books and stationery that Warner liked to browse. On this occasion there was a range of maps and she found herself buying a Bartholomew map of the English county of Essex; a place she had never visited but whose marshes and creeks as they appeared on paper in patches of green and blue enchanted her. As too, did the extraordinary names she saw marked on the map. Tracing them with her finger she delighted in the mysterious poetry of such obscure-sounding hamlets and villages as Old Shrill, High Easter, Willingale Spain and Shellow Bowells.

That August bank holiday weekend, Warner decided to discover something of Essex, and boarded a train from Fenchurch Street Station crowded with trippers heading to the resort of Southend-on-Sea, a traditional destination for working-class Londoners seeking some fun, sun and briny air beside the Thames Estuary. Warner though continued on the train to the end of the line at Shoeburyness,

where she caught a bus to Great Wakering. She had, as it happened, managed to leave her map back in Bayswater. But she remembered that 'Great Wakering was in the green section with the blue creeks' and arriving there walked out into the marshes and found a creek beyond which was a low green shore. Mesmerized by a landscape where the divisions between land and water and the soft and the solid were decidedly blurry she recalled:

> I stood there for a long time, watching the slow pushing water, and an old white horse grazing on the further shore. I followed the creek, foolishly supposing there would be some way across. It curled either way, and I began to realize that the low green shore was an island. And this again was marvellous to me, and I stood another long time, letting my mind drift with the tidal water.

By now seriously lost, she was suddenly caught up in a thunderstorm and feared being struck by lightning. Fortunately a farmer sheltering in a nearby cowshed came to her rescue. He took her home to his wife, who gave her some dry clothes to put on and cups of strong tea and fed her a hearty supper before sending Warner on her way in a pair of her daughter's heavy woollen bloomers so she wouldn't catch her death of cold.

Warner had been charmed by the whole experience. She resolved to return to Essex at the

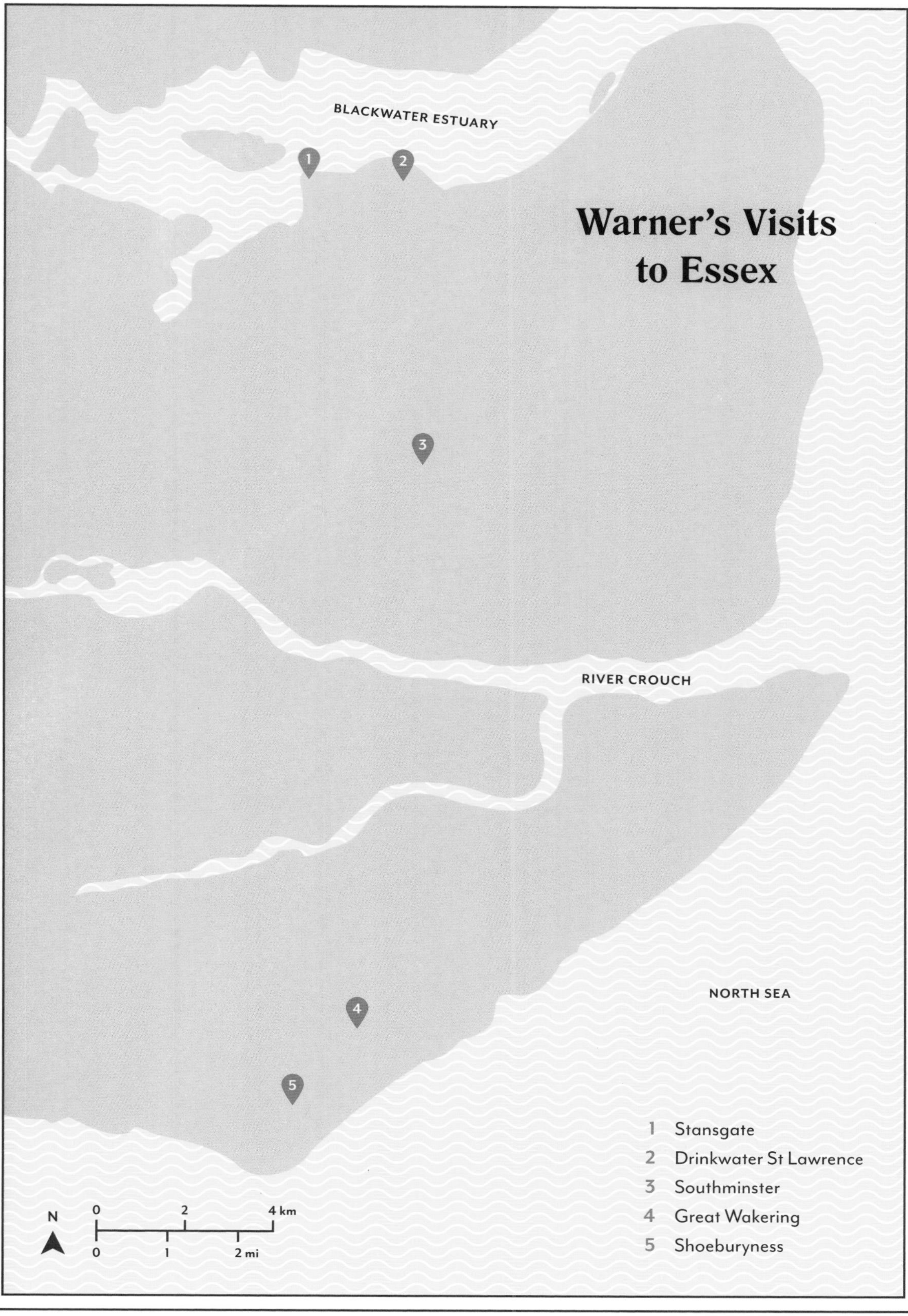

Warner's Visits to Essex

BLACKWATER ESTUARY

RIVER CROUCH

NORTH SEA

1 Stansgate
2 Drinkwater St Lawrence
3 Southminster
4 Great Wakering
5 Shoeburyness

N

| 0 | | 2 | | 4 km |
| 0 | 1 | | 2 mi | |

earliest opportunity and stay in an inn to extend the time she could spend further exploring its marshy flats and estuarine saltings. This time she departed from Liverpool Street Station for Southminster with the aim of following a path on her map to Stansgate on the Blackwater Estuary. Again she was enraptured by the almost uncanny scenery. The marsh at Blackwater was 'deeply coloured, dotted with trees, elms in clumps or sprinkled willows'. And sitting down near a small jetty running into the estuary, she was astonished to see 'the sail of a small boat moving behind some trees and seeming to move across the land'. But on consulting her map now, she discovered, that contrary to her belief, there was no inn anywhere in the vicinity. In retrospect, Warner would claim to have been 'divinely misled' for a small boy suggested she try asking a Mrs May, whose farmhouse was about half-a-mile back down the lane at Drinkwater St Lawrence, if she'd put her up for the night.

Mrs May proved more than amenable to accommodating the stranger and the pair took a liking to each other on first sight. Awakening the next morning in a spare bedroom with a large white china wash-stand that gave off a 'moony glimmer', Warner dashed to the window to look out over the Essex marsh, and watched in wonder as the farm and its outhouses, garden and orchard materialized as an all-enveloping mist melted before her eyes. Finding Mrs May downstairs, she immediately asked to stay another night.

Buoyed by the prospect of a whole day on the marshes followed by an evening in the genial company of the May family, Warner went out with her trusty map and a volume of French verse, François Villon's *Testament*. Reaching Blackwater

◀ The distant coastline of Osea
Island in the Blackwater
Estuary, Essex, England.

she sat down on a patch of grass by the estuary. As she settled down and began to read her book, glancing up occasionally to survey her surroundings, Warner experienced nothing short of an epiphany. As she subsequently put it: 'I knew that mysterious sensation of being where I wanted to be, socketed in the universe and passionately quiescent.'

Warner, in the end, was to spend a month with the Mays in the Essex marshes. During which time she drank in every aspect of the terrain, fascinated by both the scenery and the local inhabitants who included the Peculiar People, a small puritan Christian sect unique to Essex. She also made 'the discovery that it was possible to write poetry'. Warner had dabbled at writing plays and stories – her first published piece, a lengthy article entitled 'Behind the Firing Line' about her experiences of working in the Vickers munitions factory in Erith, appeared in *Blackwood's* magazine in February 1916 – but it was the Essex marshes that made her a poet and unlocked her as a writer.

Later that year she went to Blackwater for a day in the company of David 'Bunny' Garnett. Winner of the 1922 James Tait Black Memorial Prize for his novel *Lady into Fox* and a leading figure in the Bloomsbury Group, who co-owned the Birrell & Garnett Bookshop at 19 Taviton Street around the corner from the British Museum, Garnett had only recently met Warner. But on this first encounter she had spoken so enthusiastically about the beauty of the Essex marshes that Garnett had proposed they visit the Dengie Peninsula together the following Sunday. Garnett initially found plodding 'under a great sky across grey fields towards an invisible grey horizon' on a cold, grey, winter day rather less compelling than Warner. He nevertheless came to appreciate she was right, and that 'the grey marshes had a melancholy eerie beauty that was all their own'.

On a slow, cold train back to London, splattered head to toe in mud, Warner was too exhausted to talk but gave Garnett some of her poems to read. Immediately convinced of their quality, he would ensure they eventually reached Charles Prentice, an editor at Chatto & Windus. Prentice not only demanded to see more and duly published them but also asked if she might have any stories or a novel, with the result that she furnished him with a draft of *Lolly Willowes*, a book that with its dazzling account of a spinster going to the devil (quite literally) was a sensation upon its publication in 1926 and remains her best-known work today. But it was in *The True Heart*, her second novel and a reworking of the story of Cupid and Psyche, that Warner utilized the topography of Essex from her wanderings to powerful effect. Its fictionalized setting of New Easter mapping on to the curious territories that had first captivated Warner on the Barthlomew map.

▲ Portrait of David Garnett.

▶ The River Blackwater and the Essex marshes, England.

Wollstonecraft's Tour of Sweden, Norway and Denmark

1 Hull
2 Gothenburg
3 Kviström (Kvistrum)
4 Strömstad
5 Larvik (Laurvik)
6 Tønsberg
7 Oslo (Kristiania)
8 Fredrikstad
9 Trollhättan
10 Hamburg
11 Dover

NORWAY

SWEDEN

DENMARK

NORTH SEA

UNITED
KINGDOM

GERMANY

N

0   50   100 km
0   25   50 mi

Mary Wollstonecraft Soothes a Broken Heart in Scandinavia

Mary Wollstonecraft (1759–1797) departed from Hull, England, for Gothenburg, Sweden, in late June 1795. Only one month earlier, Wollstonecraft had attempted to commit suicide. The fearless author of the radical feminist text *A Vindication of the Rights of Woman* was driven to try to take her own life by an unhappy love affair with the unscrupulous American businessman Gilbert Imlay. Her decision to go to Scandinavia on Imlay's behalf and to resolve a financial matter involving a missing ship and a nefarious cargo of silver, turned (in her mind at least) on the notion of the pair being reconciled afterwards. Besides the money, for Imlay the scheme most likely had the more brutal advantage of simply getting the troublesome author out of his hair for a while. He perhaps convinced himself (mistakenly) that some time in the icy north might also help cool her ardour.

As a woman travelling with a one-year-old child and her French nursemaid in tow, Wollstonecraft made for an unlikely emissary to dispatch to the Nordic countries on business. If today Sweden, Norway and Denmark have admirable records on gender equality, the picture was considerably less rosy two hundred years ago. Wollstonecraft was to report that Swedish women were shocked and rather baffled that she should even have wanted

to go out walking alone and recounts being gently reprimanded by one of her first hosts in the country for asking 'men's questions'.

Wollstonecraft was born in Spitalfields, then an affluent suburb to the east of the City of London inhabited by large numbers of Protestant French Huguenot immigrants who worked in silk. Wollstonecraft's grandfather was a former weaver who'd prospered at the mercantile end of the trade, and the family was comfortably off at the time of the author's birth. Unfortunately, Wollstonecraft's father, Edward, a moody, capricious alcoholic, squandered their fortune pursuing the pipe-dream of becoming a gentleman farmer. In the first of a series of disastrous moves that would find them variously residing in Barking in Essex and in a village outside Beverley in the East Riding of Yorkshire, he shifted the family to Epping Forest in Essex to play at being a country squire. It was at school in Beverley that Wollstonecraft received a formative lesson in sexual inequality. While her brothers were treated to lessons in Latin, history and mathematics at the local boys' grammar school, she and her sister were taught only simple arithmetic and needlework at its neighbouring institution for girls.

In 1783 Wollstonecraft founded a progressive day school for girls with her friend Fanny Blood

in Newington Green, London; an area that also
included a Unitarian chapel where Mary herself,
along with other religious dissenters, worshipped,
and where meetings calling for political reform
and the abolition of slavery were held. Her
first published work appeared two years later.
Wollstonecraft's literary debut was to be a 162-
page pamphlet on women and pedagogy entitled
Thoughts on the Education of Daughters. Following
its positive reception, its publisher, Joseph Johnson,
agreed to keep its author supplied with batches of
reviewing and translation work, and produced all
of her subsequent books, allowing Wollstonecraft,
extremely unusually for a woman in this period, to
stop teaching and earn her living by writing alone.

Since neither writer nor publisher believed in
letting material go to waste, her Scandinavian
venture resulted in yet another book, *Letters Written
During a Short Residence in Sweden, Norway, and
Denmark*. Appearing in 1796, it was to be both the
last book published in Wollstonecraft's lifetime and
also the most critically acclaimed and commercially
successful of her career. Comprised of twenty-five
letters written to the anonymous father of her child,
the book's basis were the very real, somewhat more
emotive and occasionally downright testy private
missives that she sent to Imlay over the course of her
journey up the coast of Sweden into Norway and
then back down into Denmark on to Hamburg in
Germany, where she caught a boat back to England.

▼ Ffjord near the town of Risor
in the province of Aust-
Agder, Norway.

Leaving her daughter in the nursemaid's charge at Gothenburg for several weeks, Wollstonecraft was to visit Larvik (Laurvik), Kviström (Kvistrum) and Strömstad in Sweden before crossing into Norway and travelling to Oslo (then Kristiania), where she marvelled at the liberties enjoyed by that country's citizens under their Danish king. She was perhaps happiest in Tønsberg in Norway, where she settled for a while at the end of July and enjoyed walking, riding on horseback and swimming in the sea, and got down to writing for Johnson. Her literary endeavours here a further form of liberation from Imlay, and the fresh air and dramatic landscape a tonic to her physical and mental wellbeing.

Letters Written During a Short Residence in Sweden, Norway, and Denmark was to serve as a blueprint for a whole mode of romantic wanderings, with its first-person narrative of a forlorn, melancholy traveller spurned by her lover, journeying through remote and forbidding places. While Wollstonecraft's own emotional state is often reflected in her poetic portrayal of the rocky terrain, the book brims too with nuggets of sociological detail about the laws and customs of the Swedes, Norwegians and Danes she meets.

Wollstonecraft's descriptions of the waterfalls at Fredrikstad in Norway and Trollhättan in Sweden have been said to have provided Samuel Taylor Coleridge with the partial inspiration for his poetic rendering of the mythic river at Xanadu. And her daughter Mary Shelley's decision to send her monster-making Victor Frankenstein up into the frozen wastes of the northern hemisphere has similarly been credited with drawing on her mother's account of her excursion into the frostier parts of these territories.

It is a great tragedy that after finally extricating herself from Imlay and forming a mutually fulfilling partnership with the social philosopher and political thinker William Godwin, Wollstonecraft was to die within ten days of giving birth to Shelley. Godwin would, however, speak for many admirers of her final work in stating that, 'Perhaps a book of travels that so irresistibly seizes upon the heart of its reader never, in any other instance, found its way to the press.'

◀ **TOP** Engraving of Oslo (then Kristiania), c.1800.

◀ **BOTTOM** Engraving of Gothenburg, Sweden, c.1800.

It's All Greek to Virginia Woolf

In her 1939 essay 'A Sketch of the Past' Virginia Woolf (1882–1941) would remember that it was through her elder brother that she'd 'first heard about the Greeks'; Thoby 'Goth' Stephen regaling Woolf with the story of Hector and of Troy on his return home, for the first time, from his prep school in Hillingdon. Woolf herself went on to study Ancient Greek under George Ward in the Woman's Annexe at King's College London in 1897. And by 1902 she was receiving private lessons from the classical scholar Janet Case, whose teaching underpinned Woolf's essay on the language, 'On Not Knowing Greek'.

In September 1906 Woolf was to travel to Greece for the first time in the company of her sister Vanessa and Violet Dickinson, an older, intimate family friend. Thoby and her youngest sibling, Adrian, who they'd arranged to meet in Olympia, had gone ahead already. Woolf prepared for the trip by poring over maps and guidebooks, attempting to unpick quite where the classical country of her learning and imagination lay geographically in relation to the modern Greek nation established after centuries of Ottoman rule.

Virginia, Vanessa and Violet went first by train through Italy to Brindisi. A boat then carried them to Patras in Greece, where they boarded an extremely dilatory train to Olympia. Woolf was left reeling by the idea that a railway station and the site of the Ancient Greek statue of Hermes of Praxiteles could exist in the same vicinity.

As her biographer Hermione Lee makes clear, Woolf was, for the most part, somewhat nonplussed by the contemporary Hellenic world. The bed bugs in their hotel in Corinth and the beggars all contributed to her negative responses. The modern bits of Athens, and the modern Athenians 'who didn't understand Ancient Greek', Lee notes, Woolf judged 'unAthenian'. Elsewhere and in her diary, she was to maintain that modern Greece was 'so flimsy and fragile' that it went to 'pieces entirely when … confronted with the roughest fragments of the old'.

But Athens' more august quarters, with their narrow streets, put her in mind of St Ives in Cornwall, where she had spent much of her childhood. The Acropolis, which she'd written in letters beforehand of yearning to cross Europe to clamber atop, couldn't really disappoint. And in her 1922 novel *Jacob's Room*, parts of which are set in Greece, she evoked the view, writing, 'the sight of Hymettus, Pentilcus, Lycabettus on one side, and the sea on the other, as one stands in the Parthenon at sunset, the sky pink feathered, the plain all colours, the marble tawny in one's eyes, is thus oppressive'.

Several incidents from this Greek trip, including an expedition by mule up Mount Pentelicus, were to find their way into her debut novel of 1915, *The Voyage Out*, despite the book ostensibly being about a group of English passengers sailing for South America.

Woolf's tour of historic sites would go on to encompass Eleusis, the fort at Nafplion (Nauplia),

the amphitheatre at Epidaurus and the great tombs at Mycenae and in Tiryns, the 'Homeric palace' which she judged 'like an English Castle, only pre-historic', while at Achmetaga on Euboea she observed archaeologists at work on the ruins. From Euboea, the party caught a boat and sailed through the Dardanelles to Istanbul (then Constantinople), where they looked in on the evening worshippers at the Hagia Sophia.

Vanessa had been sick for most of their time in Greece, having come down with appendicitis on the voyage over, and spent most of the trip confined to her hotel room under Violet's care in Athens, while Virginia and the others ventured further afield. On 14 October, Thoby left for London. The remainder of the party, and despite Vanessa's ill health, chose a more leisurely passage home, travelling on the Orient Express train from Istanbul to Ostend in Belgium, and then sailing by ferry to Dover in England, where they landed on 1 November 1906.

Back in London, though, they were to discover that Thoby was suffering with an appalling fever and diarrhoea. Their family doctor at first diagnosed malaria but when the patient continued to deteriorate it was finally realized that he had typhoid. The prognosis was at first good but after an operation on 17 November things went from bad to worse, and he died just three days later, aged only twenty-six.

1	Patras
2	Olympia
3	Mycenae
4	Tiryns
5	Nafplion (Nauplia)
6	Corinth
7	Epidaurus
8	Eleusis
9	Athens
10	Achmetaga
11	Euboea

GREECE

Woolf's Tour of Greece

◀ PREVIOUS PAGE Acropolis of Athens.

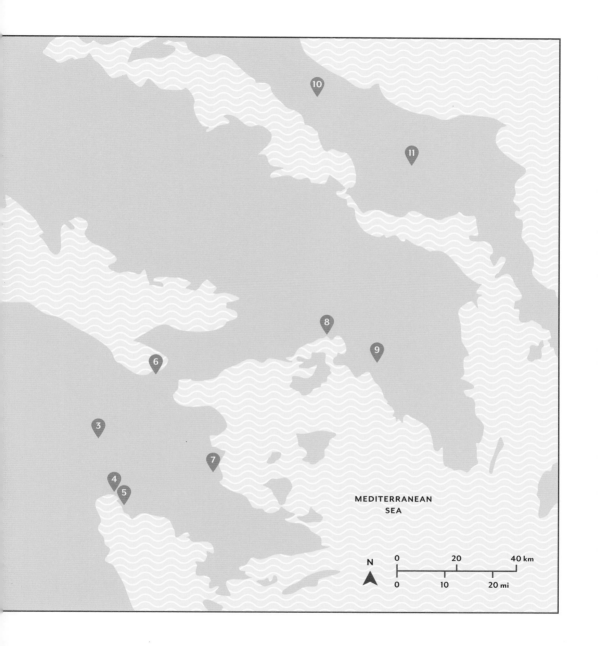

MEDITERRANEAN
SEA

N

0		20		40 km
0	10		20 mi	

As the initiator of regular Thursday evening gatherings of like-minded friends at the Stephens' London home, Thoby can justly be claimed as the progenitor of the Bloomsbury Group of writers and artists. Woolf would go on to venerate her brother's memory, and their time in Greece together, in her writing. *Jacob's Room*, in particular, was composed as an elegy for Thoby; its namesake sharing many of his circumstances and characteristics.

◀ Watercolour painting of the Theatre of Epidaurus, Greece, c.1906.

▼ Portrait of Thoby Stephen, c.1902.

Selected Bibliography

This book owes an enormous debt to numerous other books and articles. This select bibliography will, hopefully, give credit where credit is due and point those who want to know more in the right directions.

Hans Christian Andersen

Andersen, Jens, *Hans Christian Andersen: A New Life*, trans. Tina Nunnally (Duckworth, 2006).

Binding, Paul, *Hans Christian Andersen: European Witness* (Yale University Press, 2014).

Godden, Rumer, *Hans Christian Andersen* (Hutchinson, 1955).

Maya Angelou

Angelou, Maya, *All God's Children Need Traveling Shoes* (Random House, 1986).

Lubabu, Tshitenge, 'Maya Angelou's Meeting with Africa', *The Africa Report*, 16 December 2011, https://www.theafricareport.com/7921/maya-angelous-meeting-with-africa/.

W.H. Auden and Christopher Isherwood

Auden, W.H. and Christopher Isherwood, *The Ascent of F6*, (Faber, 1936).

Auden, W.H. and Christopher Isherwood, *Journey to a War*, (Faber, 1939).

Carpenter, Humphrey, *W.H. Auden: A Biography* (Allen & Unwin, 1981).

Fryer, Jonathan, *Isherwood: A Biography of Christopher Isherwood* (New English Library, 1977).

Isherwood, Christopher, *Christopher and His Kind*, 1929–1939 (Methuen, 1985).

Parker, Peter, *Isherwood: A Life* (Picador, 2004).

Jane Austen

Austen, Jane, *Sanditon*, ed. Kathryn Sutherland (Oxford University Press, 2019).

Cecil, David, *A Portrait of Jane Austen* (Penguin, 2000).

Edwards, Antony, *Jane Austen's Worthing: The Real Sanditon* (Amberley, 2013).

Elborough, Travis, *Wish You Were Here: England on Sea* (Sceptre, 2010).

Noakes, David, *Jane Austen: A Life* (Fourth Estate, 1997).

Tomalin, Claire, *Jane Austen: A Life* (Viking, 1997).

James Baldwin

Campbell, James, *Talking at the Gates: A Life of James Baldwin* (Faber, 1991).

Leeming, David Adams, *James Baldwin: A Biography*, (Michael Joseph, 1994).

Miller, D. Quentin, ed., *James Baldwin in Context* (Cambridge University Press, 2019).

Washington, Ellery, 'James Baldwin's Paris', *The New York Times*, 17 January 2017, https://www.nytimes.com/2014/01/19/travel/james-baldwins-paris.html.

Bashō

Barnhill, David Landis, *Basho's Journey: The Literary Prose of Matsuo Basho* (State University of New York Press, 2005).

Bashō , Matsuo, *Basho's Narrow Road: Spring & Autumn Passage*, trans. Hiroaki Sato (Stone Bridge, 1996).

Bashō, Matsuo, *The Narrow Road to the Deep North and Other Travel Sketches*, trans. Nobuyuki Yuasa (Penguin, 2005).

Downer, Lesley, *On the Narrow Road to the Deep North: Journey Into a Lost Japan* (Jonathan Cape, 1989).

Charles Baudelaire

Hemmings, F.W.J., *Baudelaire The Damned: A Biography* (Hamish Hamilton, 1982).

Hyslop, Lois Boe, *Baudelaire, Man of His Time* (Yale University Press, 1980).

Morgan, Edwin, *Flower of Evil: A Life of Charles Baudelaire* (Sheed & Ward, 1944).

Elizabeth Bishop

Bishop, Elizabeth, *Brazil* (*The Sunday Times*, World Library, 1963).

Bishop, Elizabeth, *The Complete Poems* (Chatto & Windus, 1970).

Goldensohn, Lorrie, *Elizabeth Bishop: The Biography of a Poetry* (Columbia University Press, 1992).

Marshall, Megan, *Elizabeth Bishop: A Miracle for Breakfast* (Houghton Mifflin Harcourt, 2017).

Miller, Brett, *Elizabeth Bishop: Life and the Memory of It* (University of California Press, 1993).

Travisano, Thomas, *Love Unknown: The Life and Worlds of Elizabeth Bishop* (Viking, 2019).

Heinrich Böll

Böll, Heinrich, *Irish Journal* (Secker & Warburg, 1983).

Holfter, Gisela, *Heinrich Böll and Ireland* (Cambridge Scholars Publishing, 2011).

O'Toole, Fintan, 'We Must All Learn the Art of Political Dentistry', *The Irish Times*, 20 April 2019.

Reid, J.H., *Heinrich Böll: A German for His Time* (Oswald Wolff, 1988).

Lewis Carroll

Amor, Anne Clark, *Lewis Carroll: A Biography* (Dent, 1979).

Bakewell, Michael, *Lewis Carroll: A Biography* (Heinemann, 1996).

Carroll, Lewis, *The Russian Journal, and Other Selections from the Works of Lewis Carroll*, ed. John Francis McDermott (E.P. Dutton & Co, 1935).

Cohen, Morton N., *Lewis Carroll : A Biography* (Macmillan, 1995).

Agatha Christie

Burton, Anthony, *The Orient Express: The History of the Orient-Express Service from 1883 to 1950* (Chartwell Books, 2001).

Christie, Agatha, *An Autobiography* (Collins, 1977).

Christie, Agatha, *Murder on the Orient Express* (HarperCollins, 2006).

Martin, Andrew, *Night Trains: The Rise and Fall of the Sleeper* (Profile, 2008).

Morgan, Janet, *Agatha Christie: A Biography* (Collins, 1984).

Wilkie Collins and Charles Dickens

Collins, Wilkie and Charles Dickens, *The Lazy Tour of Two Idle Apprentices. No Thoroughfare. The Perils of Certain English Prisoners* (Chapman & Hall, 1890).

Lycett, Andrew, *Wilkie Collins: A Life of Sensation* (Hutchinson, 2013).

Nayder, Lillian, *Unequal Partners: Charles Dickens, Wilkie Collins, and Victorian Authorship* (Cornell University Press, 2002).

Tomalin, Claire, *Charles Dickens: A Life* (Viking, 2011).

Wilson, A.N., *The Mystery of Charles Dickens* (Atlantic Books, 2020).

Joseph Conrad

Batchelor, John, *The Life of Joseph Conrad: A Critical Biography* (Blackwell, 1994).

Conrad, Joseph, *Heart of Darkness and Other Tales* (Oxford University Press, 2002).

Conrad, Joseph, *Last Essays* (Cambridge University Press, 2010).

Meyers, Jeffrey, *Joseph Conrad: A Biography* (John Murray, 1991).

Isak Dinesen

Dinesen, Isak, *Letters from Africa, 1914–1931* (Weidenfeld and Nicolson, 1981).

Dinesen, Isak, *Out of Africa* (Random House, 1938).

Hannah, Donald, *Isak Dinesen and Karen Blixen: The Mask and The Reality* (Putnam & Company, 1971).

Thurman, Judith, *Isak Dinesen: The Life of Karen Blixen* (Weidenfeld and Nicolson, 1982).

Sir Arthur Conan Doyle

Booth, Martin, *The Doctor, the Detective and Arthur Conan Doyle: A Biography of Arthur Conan Doyle* (Coronet, 1998).

Brown, Ivor John Carnegie, *Conan Doyle: A biography of the Creator of Sherlock Holmes* (Hamilton, 1972).

Doyle, Arthur Conan, *Memories and Adventures* (Hodder and Stoughton, 1924).

Doyle, Arthur Conan, *The Penguin Complete Sherlock Holmes* (Penguin Books, 2009).

Rennison, Nick, *Sherlock Holmes: The Unauthorized Biography* (Atlantic, 2005).

Ring, Jim, *How the English Made the Alps* (John Murray, 2000).

Sims, Michael, *Arthur & Sherlock: Conan Doyle and the Creation of Holmes* (Bloomsbury, 2017).

F. Scott Fitzgerald

Brown, David S., *Paradise Lost: A Life of F. Scott Fitzgerald* (The Belknap Press of Harvard University Press, 2017).

Churchwell, Sarah, *Careless People: Murder, Mayhem and The Invention of The Great Gatsby* (Virago, 2013).

Elborough, Travis, *Wish You Were Here: England on Sea* (Sceptre, 2010).

Fitzgerald, F. Scott, *The Bodley Head Scott Fitzgerald, vol. ii: Autobiographical Pieces, Letters to Frances Scott Fitzgerald, Tender is the Night and Short Stories* (The Bodley Head, 1959).

Grand, Xavier, *The French Riviera in the 1920s* (Assouline Publishing, 2014).

Meyer, Jeffrey, *Scott Fitzgerald: A Biography* (Macmillan, 1994).

Vaill, Amanda, *Everybody Was So Young: Gerald and Sara Murphy, a Lost Generation Love Story* (Little, Brown, 1998).

Gustave Flaubert

Sattin, Anthony, *A Winter on the Nile: Florence Nightingale, Gustave Flaubert and the Temptations of Egypt* (Hutchinson, 2010).

Steegmuller, Francis, *Flaubert in Egypt: A Sensibility on Tour: A Narrative Drawn from Gustave Flaubert's Travel Notes & Letters* (The Bodley Head, 1972).

Wall, Geoffrey, *Flaubert: A Life* (Faber, 2001).

Johann Wolfgang von Goethe

Goethe, Johann Wolfgang von, *Italian Journey, 1786–1788* (Collins, 1962).

Hamilton, Paul, ed., *The Oxford Handbook of European Romanticism* (Oxford University Press, 2016).

Reed, T.J., *Goethe* (Oxford University Press, 1984).

Safranski, Rüdiger, *Goethe: Life As a Work of Art*, trans. David B. Dollenmayer (Liveright Publishing Corporation/W.W. Norton & Company, 2017).

Williams, John R., *The Life of Goethe: A Critical Biography* (Blackwell, 1998).

Graham Greene

Butcher, Tim, *Chasing the Devil: a Journey Through Sub-Saharan Africa in the Footsteps of Graham Greene* (Atlas & Co. Publishers, 2011).

Greene, Barbara, *Too Late to Turn Back: Barbara and Graham Greene in Liberia* (Settle Bendall, 1981).

Greene, Graham, *Journey Without Maps* (Heinemann, Bodley Head, 1978).

Sherry, Norman, *The Life of Graham Greene, vol. i, 1904–1939* (Penguin, 1990).

Hermann Hesse

Decker, Gunnar, *Hesse: The Wanderer and His Shadow*, trans. Peter Lewis (Harvard University Press, 2018).

Freedman, Ralph, *Hermann Hesse: Pilgrim of Crisis: A Biography* (Jonathan Cape, 1979).

Hesse, Hermann, *Autobiographical Writings*, trans. and eds. Denver Lindley and Theodore Ziolkowski (Jonathan Cape, 1973).

Hesse, Hermann, *The Journey to the East* (Peter Owen, 1964).

Hesse, Hermann, *Siddhartha* (Peter Owen, 1954).

Varghese Reji, 'An Indian Tale', *The Hindu*, 1 July 2015, https://www.thehindu.com/features/metroplus/on-hermann-hesses-birth-anniversary-an-indian-tale/article7374743.ece.

Patricia Highsmith

Wilson, Andrew, *Beautiful Shadow: A Life of Patricia Highsmith* (Bloomsbury, 2003).

Wilson, Andrew, 'Italian Holidays: Talent Shows', *The Guardian*, 15 October 2005, https://www.theguardian.com/travel/2005/oct/15/italy.onlocationfilminspiredtravel.guardiansaturdaytravelsection.

Zora Neale Hurston

Boys, Valerie, *Wrapped in Rainbows: The Life of Zora Neale Hurston* (Virago, 2003).

Duck, Leigh Anne, 'Rebirth of a Nation: Hurston in Haiti', *The Journal of American Folklore*, vol. 117, no. 464 (Spring, 2004) pp.127–146, University of Illinois Press, https://www.jstor.org/stable/4137818.

Hurston, Zora Neale, *Voodoo Gods: An Inquiry Into Native Myths and Magic in Jamaica and Haiti* (J.M. Dent & Sons, 1939).

Plant, Deborah G., *Zora Neale Hurston: A Biography of the Spirit* (Praeger, 2007).

Jack Kerouac

Charters, Ann, *Kerouac: A Biography* (Deutsch, 1974).

Johnson, Joyce, *Minor Characters* (Methuen, 2012).

Kerouac, Jack, *Selected Letters, 1940–1956*, ed. Ann Charters (Viking, 1995).

Maher, Paul, *Jack Kerouac's American Journey: The Real-life Odyssey of 'On the Road'* (Thunder's Mouth Press, 2007).

Maher, Paul, *Kerouac: The Definitive Biography* (Taylor Trade, 2004).

Miles, Barry, *Jack Kerouac, King of the Beats: A Portrait, London* (Virgin Books, 1998).

Nicosia, Gerald, *Memory Babe: A Critical Biography of Jack Kerouac* (Grove Press, 1983).

Jack London

Kershaw, Alex, *Jack London: A Life* (Harper Collins, 1997).

Labor, Earle, *Jack London: An American Life* (Farrar, Straus & Giroux, 2013).

Sinclair, Andrew, *Jack: A Biography of Jack London* (Weidenfeld and Nicolson, 1978).

Stone, Irving, *Sailor on Horseback: The Biography of Jack London* (Houghton Mifflin, 1938).

Federico García Lorca

Gibson, Ian, *Federico García Lorca: A Life* (Faber, 1989).

Lorca, Federico García, *Poet in New York*, trans. Ben Belitt (Thames and Hudson, 1955).

McLane, Maureen, N., 'On Lorca's Poet in New York', FSG Work in Progress, https://fsgworkinprogress. com/2013/04/18/on-lorcas-poet-in-new-york.

Stainton, Leslie, *Lorca: A Dream of Life* (Bloomsbury, 1998).

Katherine Mansfield

Kimber, Gerri, *Katherine Mansfield: The Early Years* (Edinburgh University Press, 2016).

Mansfield, Katherine, *In a German Pension* (Constable, 1926).

Meyers, Jeffery, *Katherine Mansfield: A Biography* (Hamish Hamilton, 1978).

Murry, John Middleton, *Katherine Mansfield and Other Literary Portraits* (Peter Nevill, 1949).

Tomalin, Claire, *Katherine Mansfield: A Secret Life* (Viking, 1987).

Herman Melville

Allen, Gay Wilson, *Melville and His World* (Thames and Hudson, 1971).

Delbanco, Andrew, *Melville: His World and Work* (London: Picador, 2005).

Gilman, W.H., *Melville's Early Life and Redburn* (Russell & Russell, 1972).

Hoare, Philip, *Leviathan, or the Whale* (Fourth Estate, 2008).

Lawrence, D.H., *Studies in Classic American Literature* (Heinemann, 1964).

Meville, Herman, *Redburn: His First Voyage; White-Jacket, or, The World in a Man-of-War; Moby-Dick, or, The Whale* (Tanselle, G. Thomas, Literary Classics of the United States America, 1983).

Alexandr Pushkin

Binyon, T.J., *Pushkin: A Biography* (HarperCollins, 2002).

Feinstein, Elaine, *Pushkin* (Weidenfeld and Nicolson, 1998).

Magarshack, David, *Pushkin: A Biography* (Chapman & Hall, 1967).

Pushkin, Aleksandr Sergeevich, *A Journey to Arzrum*, trans. Birgitta Ingemanson (Ardis, 1974).

Vitale, Serena, *Pushkin's Button* (Fourth Estate, 1999).

J.K. Rowling

'J.K. Rowling: Harry Potter and Me', BBC Omnibus documentary, 2001, directed by Nicky Pattison.

Antoine de Saint-Exupéry

Cate, Cutis, *Antoine de Saint-Exupéry: His Life and Times* (Heinemann, 1970).

Saint-Exupéry, Antoine de, *Wind, Sand and Stars* (Penguin Books, 2000).

Schiff, Stacy, *Saint-Exupéry: A Biography* (Chatto & Windus, 1994).

Sam Selvon

Bentley, Nick, 'Black London: The Politics of Representation in Sam Selvon's *The Lonely Londoners*', *Wasafiri*, 2003, 18:39, pp.41–45, https://doi.org/10.1080/02690050308589846.

Dawson, Ashley, *Mongrel Nation: Diasporic Culture and the Making of Postcolonial Britain* (Michigan Publishing/University of Michigan, 2007).

James, Louis, 'Obituary: Sam Selvon', *The Independent*, 19 April 1994.

Lamming, George, *The Pleasures of Exile* (Allison & Busby, 1981).

Sandhu, Sukhdev, *London Calling: How Black and Asian Writers Imagined a City* (HarperCollins, 2003).

Selvon, Samuel, *A Brighter Sun* (Longman, 1979).

Selvon, Samuel, *The Lonely Londoners* (Penguin, 2006).

Bram Stoker

Belford, Barbara, *Bram Stoker: A Biography of the Author of Dracula* (Weidenfeld and Nicolson, 1996).

Farson, Daniel, *The Man Who Wrote Dracula: A Biography of Bram Stoker* (Michael Joseph, 1975).

Frayling, Christopher, *Vampyres: Genesis and Resurrection from Count Dracula to Vampirella* (Thames & Hudson, 2016).

Murray, Paul, *From the Shadow of Dracula: A Life of Bram Stoker* (Cape, 2004).

Stoker, Bram, *The Annotated Dracula: Dracula*, ed. Leonard Wolf (New English, 1976).

Sylvia Townsend Warner

Harman, Claire, *Sylvia Townsend Warner: A Biography* (Chatto & Windus, 1989).

Warner, Sylvia Townsend, *Letters* (Chatto & Windus, 1982).

Warner, Sylvia Townsend, *The True Heart* (Chatto & Windus, 1929).

Worpole, Ken, 'The Peculiar People', *The New English Landscape*, 6 January 2014, https://thenewenglishlandscape.wordpress.com/tag/sylvia-townsend-warner-the-true-heart/.

Mary Wollstonecraft

Jacobs, Diane, *Her Own Woman: The life of Mary Wollstonecraft* (Abacus, 2001).

Sampson, Fiona, *In Search of Mary Shelley: the Girl Who Wrote Frankenstein* (Profile Books, 2018).

Spufford, Francis, *I May Be Some Time: Ice and the English Imagination* (Faber, 1996).

Tomalin, Claire, *The Life and Death of Mary Wollstonecraft* (Weidenfeld and Nicolson, 1974).

Williams, John, *Mary Shelley: A Literary Life* (Macmillan, 2000).

Wollstonecraft, Mary, *Letters Written in Sweden, Norway, and Denmark* (Oxford World's Classics, 2009).

Virginia Woolf

Bell, Quentin, *Virginia Woolf: A Biography* (Hogarth Press, 1982).

Fowler, Rowena, 'Moments and Metamorphoses: Virginia Woolf's Greece', *Comparative Literature* vol. 51, no. 3 (Summer, 1999), pp.217–242, Duke University Press, https://www.jstor.org/stable/1771668.

Koulouris, Theodore, *Hellenism and Loss in the Work of Virginia Woolf* (Routledge, Taylor & Francis Group, 2018).

Lee, Hermione, *Virginia Woolf* (Chatto & Windus, 1996).

Pippett, Aileen, *The Moth and the Star: A Biography of Virginia Woolf* (Little, Brown, 1955).

Woolf, Virginia, *Moments of Being: Unpublished Autobiographical*, ed. Jeanne Schulkind (Chatto and Windus for Sussex University Press, 1976).

Index

Picture Credits

2 Peter Fogden/Unsplash; 9 Wjaceslav Polejaev/Dreamstime; 11 above Carlos Ibáñez/Unsplash; 11 below Niday Picture Library/Alamy Stock Photo; 12 Andrew Pinder; 14 Virgyl Sowah/Unsplash; 15 Ariadne Van Zandbergen/Alamy Stock Photo; 17 Andrew Pinder; 18 Bettmann/Getty Images; 19 Kaiyu Wu/Unsplash; 20–1 Yang Song/Unsplash; 22 Ivona17/Dreamstime; 25 Look and Learn/Illustrated Papers Collection/Bridgeman Images; 26–7 Trigger Image/Alamy Stock Photo; 28 Adrien/Unsplash; 29 Andrew Pinder; 32 Robert Doisneau/Gamma-Rapho/Getty Images; 33 Keystone-France/Gamma-Rapho/Getty Images; 34 CPA Media Pte Ltd/Alamy Stock Photo; 37 David Bertho/Alamy Stock Photo; 39 German Vizulis/Shutterstock; 40–1 Old Images/Alamy Stock Photo; 42–3 Xavier Coiffic/Unsplash; 44 Andrew Pinder; 45 BrazilPhotos/Alamy Stock Photo; 48 Leonardo Finotti; 49 Imagebroker/Alamy Stock Photo; 50 Rizby Mazumder/Unsplash; 51 Andrew Pinder; 54 Ivona17/Dreamstime; 55 Christian Wiediger/Unsplash; 58–9 iam_os/Unsplash; 60 Shawshots/Alamy Stock Photo; 61 Ivona17/Dreamstime; 64–5 robertharding/Alamy Stock Photo; 66 Daniel Burka/Unsplash; 68 Andrew Pinder; 70 Gavin Dronfield/Alamy Stock Photo; 71 above Illustrated London News Ltd/Mary Evans; 71 below Hulton Archive/Getty Images; 73 Granger Historical Picture Archive/Alamy Stock Photo; 74 EyeEm/Alamy Stock Photo; 75 DeAgostini/Biblioteca Ambrosiana/Getty Images; 76–7 Zute Lightfoot/Alamy Stock Photo; 78 Andrew Pinder; 80 Apic/Getty Images; 81 DeAgostini/G. Wright/Getty Images; 82 Ivona17/Dreamstime; 84–5 Marc/Unsplash; 86 Hulton Archive/Getty Images; 88–9 eugen_z/Alamy Stock Photo; 90 Andrew Pinder; 91 Michael Shannon/Unsplash; 94 Christie's Images/Bridgeman Images; 95 Photo12/Universal Images Group/Getty Images; 96–7 Gerti Gjuzi/Unsplash; 99 Ivona17/Dreamstime; 100–101 Omar Elsharawy/Unsplash; 103 Granger/Bridgeman Images; 104 Ivona17/Dreamstime; 106 DeAgostini/Getty Images; 107 Henrique Ferreira/Unsplash; 108 DeAgostini/Getty Images; 109 Anastasiia Rozumna/Unsplash; 110–11 Anjuna Ale/Unsplash; 112 Social Income/Unsplash; 113 Andrew Pinder; 116–17 Tommy Trenchard/Alamy Stock Photo; 117 sjbooks/Alamy Stock Photo; 118 Ivona17/Dreamstime; 119 Alex Azabache/Unsplash; 122 VTR/Alamy Stock Photo; 123 above Hulton Archive/Getty Images; 123 below Kenishirotie/Alamy Stock Photo; 125 Andrew Pinder; 127 Samuel C./Unsplash; 128–9 Letizia Agosta/Unsplash; 130 Yves Alarie/Unsplash; 131 Andrew Pinder; 132 Everett Collection/Bridgeman Images; 135 J.B. Helsby/Topical Press Agency/Getty Images; 136 Andrew Pinder; 137 Jean Colet/Unsplash; 138 above Private Collection/Bridgeman Images; 138 below Jason Finn/Alamy Stock Photo; 141 Robert Gomez/Unsplash; 143 Naci Yavuz/Shutterstock; 145 Kayti Coonjohn; 146 Stefano Bianchetti/Corbis/Getty Images; 147 Christophel Fine Art/Universal Images Group/Getty Images; 149 Andrew Pinder; 150 Bettmann/Getty Images; 151 Zach Miles/Unsplash; 152–3 Kumar Sriskandan/Alamy Stock Photo; 154 Sam Oaksey/Alamy Stock Photo; 156–7 NatureQualityPicture/Shutterstock; 158 ullstein bild/ullstein bild/Getty Images; 159 Look and Learn/Valerie Jackson Harris Collection/Bridgeman Images; 160 Phil Kiel/Unsplash; 161 German Vizulis/Shutterstock; 165 Peacock Graphics/Alamy Stock Photo; 166 T. Latysheva/Shutterstock; 168 Lena Serditova/Shutterstock; 170 Artepics/Alamy Stock Photo; 171 Fine Art Images/Heritage Images/Getty Images; 172 thongyhod/Shutterstock; 174 Shahid Khan/Alamy Stock Photo; 175 Sarah Ehlers/Unsplash; 177 Andrew Pinder; 178–9 Michele Burgess/Alamy Stock Photo; 180 Spaarnestad Photo/Bridgeman Images; 181 Keystone Press/Alamy Stock Photo; 182 Andrew Pinder; 183 Pierre Becam/Unsplash; 186 The National Archives/SSPL/Getty Images; 187 Daily Express/Pictorial Parade/Hulton Archive/Getty Images; 188 Jess McMahon/Unsplash; 189 Private Collection; 192 Paul Williams/Alamy Stock Photo; 193 steeve-x-foto/Alamy Stock Photo; 194 Andrew Pinder; 196–7 G. Scammell/Alamy Stock Photo; 198 Bridgeman Images; 199 Daniel Jones/Alamy Stock Photo; 201 Andrew Pinder; 202–3 mariusz.ks/Shutterstock; 204 above Universal History Archive/Universal Images Group/Getty Images; 204 below Universal History Archive/Universal Images Group/Getty Images; 206 Andrew Pinder; 207 Pat Whelen/Unsplash; 210–11 Niday Picture Library/Alamy Stock Photo; 211 Bridgeman Images.

Author Acknowledgments

Thanks to Zara Anvari who commissioned this book, Clare Churly for her diligent editing of the manuscript and much else besides and Michael Brunstrom for further editorial input on its contents and the final text. This book could hardly dare to be called an atlas without its maps, which, along with the cover art, were drawn by Hannah Naughton. And thanks too to Andrew Pinder for his marvellous illustrations.

Further thanks to Richard Green, Jessica Axe, Katie Bond and everyone at White Lion and Aurum for their efforts on behalf of this book and previous atlases, and especially Melody Odusanya for publicity.

Thanks to the staff and librarians at The British Library in St Pancras, The London Library in St James's and Hackney Libraries, Stoke Newington branch.

And in addition I'd like to thank friends (ancient and modern and absent and present), my folks and family on either side of the Atlantic and my brilliant and beautiful wife, Emily Bick, and our cats Hilda and Kit.

Brimming with creative inspiration, how-to projects, and useful information to enrich your everyday life, quarto.com is a favourite destination for those pursuing their interests and passions.

First published in 2022 by White Lion Publishing an imprint of The Quarto Group.
The Old Brewery, 6 Blundell Street,
London N7 9BH,
United Kingdom.
T (0)20 7700 6700
www.Quarto.com

Copyright © 2022 Quarto Publishing plc
Text © 2022 Travis Elborough
Photographs and illustrations © as listed on page 223

Commissioning editor: Zara Anvari
Project editor: Clare Churly
Design and maps: Hannah Naughton

A catalogue record for this book is available from the British Library.

ISBN 978-0-7112-6872-2
eBook ISBN 978-0-7112-6874-6

10 9 8 7 6 5 4 3 2 1

Typeset in Mr Eaves Modern and Romana

Printed and bound in Singapore

MIX
Paper from responsible sources
FSC™ C007207